carpercommunications.com

Design by RedTree Web Design

Table of Contents

FOREWORD

I don't get much sleep, and here's one of the big reasons why: the world is full of brilliant ideas and talented people and remarkable products that no one will ever hear about. Ever. For every breakout YouTube star there are 10,000 people that are just as good or better that only have a handful of views. For every Thomas Edison, there is a Nikola Tesla toiling away in obscurity. This is a problem across the full spectrum of humanity–musicians, artists, writers, inventors, designers, builders, craftsman, programmers. I think about the people and the brands that inspire me, and then I imagine how many amazing things are out there that I–or anyone else–will never hear about.

And then I don't sleep.

Our world has no shortage of amazing people and ideas. Instead, our problem is that creators are often not marketers. Producing a worthwhile piece of art or creating an effective product is a difficult process in its own right that requires a great deal of insight and skill. Demanding that this person then become a master of promotion is unfair.

If someone makes the best cheeseburger in the world, they should be able to focus on making cheeseburgers, and that's better for the person that eats the cheeseburgers too. As soon as that same individual has to step back and run their business, they are forced to think a lot less about the perfect cheese and the ideal temperature and that new aging process they want to try and instead are forced to make sense of why their restaurant is losing revenue while the chain restaurant down the street is packed every night.

These are the people I love to help because it feels like some form of poetic justice when the community at large finally learns how awesome the business tucked in the corner of some business park really is. I wrote this book for that reason. I want more business owners and creators to have a fair shot at being heard, so I am going to walk you through the process that I use every day with my clients to find innovative ways to connect with the audience best suited for your product or service.

When I say innovation, I mean it. The reason that so many businesses struggle to gain traction with their marketing is because they think that they have to compete the way everyone else competes. That's a trap that your established competitors want you to fall into because it's a fight they know they can win.

No more. We are going to blaze a new trail that moves you out of obscurity and puts you in front of your audience in a way that your competitors will struggle to emulate.

1

THE INNOVATIVE BRAND

One of the first pieces of advice entrepreneurs often hear is "find your niche." This wisdom is sound. If you want to attract new customers, you have to be different from the competitors in your space. An established business has a loyal following, and unless they are treating their customers poorly, the existing relationship a customer has will trump the shiny untested newness of an emerging brand.

Entire books have been written on this topic, and many of them are worth reading, but here is an overview of some ways that innovative businesses use this niche philosophy to set themselves apart in competitive markets:

- **Improve features.** They offer a product that is similar to other products but performs better or offers additional impactful functionality.
- **Shift target audiences.** The product itself might not change much, but the brand taps into a new target audience.
- **Address new problems.** An evolving industry often means new pain points that a young company can solve.
- **Create a new market.** Introduce an entirely new product type that the audience didn't know it wanted.

Admittedly, this is an extremely generalized summary of what should be an in-depth, time-intensive process. Identifying your niche and designing your business accordingly is one of the first make-or-break moments a business owner experiences.

It should not be taken lightly and should be given the appropriate amount of time and research.

For my part as a marketer, I often talk with business owners who passionately discuss their unique niches. They understand how important a niche is, but when it comes to their marketing strategy, the niche philosophy disappears. They reduce their businesses to competing on the same platforms and in the same ways as everyone else in their space.

As a result, they fail to meaningfully communicate what makes their product or service different.

It's a heartbreaking reality, but how it comes to pass is understandable. Business owners intuitively understand their industries and their place within them. They can talk specs and data and history and trends. But they haven't devoted the same energy and time to understanding effective marketing strategy.

That's the gap this book aims to close. I will give you a process for designing and executing a marketing strategy that matches the uniqueness of your business.

Front Door Static

The same reasoning that informs defining the niche for your business applies to your marketing. If you choose to compete along the same avenues and with the same approaches as well-established competitors, you are setting yourself up for failure. Here's why:

- When you do the same thing as everyone else, you won't standout.
- Available space or air-time is limited because all of your competitors want it too.
- The demand for these popular channels makes using them costlier.
- The momentum of existing brands in these channels gives them an advantage.
- The audiences connected to popular channels can become less receptive to new messages because of message-fatigue.

I think of non-niche marketing as a crowded front door. When everyone is trying to push through a single choke point, very few actually make it to the other side. In the business world, the people that get through are often the ones that have some sort of VIP pass or a big enough budget to steamroll everyone in their way. For an underdog, this is a tough proposition. How different you are and how effective your product is become irrelevant if no one can hear you talk about it.

To engage your target audience, you have to approach your marketing strategy with the niche philosophy. Just as you wouldn't exactly duplicate a competitor's business model, you shouldn't exactly duplicate their marketing approach either.

Be different.

Sure, that's easy enough to say, but it's really difficult to do. I've spent the last 10 years refusing to compete on the same terms as established brands, whether that's in my own businesses or in the advice that I give to clients. I don't mean that we abandon traditional marketing channels. We keep all of the same options on the table–billboards, pay-per-click ads, radio, Facebook ads, whatever–but we identify what our competition is doing and make the deliberate choice to not use the same tools in the same way.

At the risk of beating a dead horse, let's take Apple as an example.

The vast majority of electronics companies distribute through a third party. Dell, HP, Samsung, Toshiba, Asus and so on don't have their own chain of physical stores. They sell through retailers like Best Buy. Apple decided that they didn't want to compete exclusively in third party retail channels, so they designed their own dedicated stores and crafted an experience that was distinctly different from that of a big box store

An Apple store is unlike any other electronics store. In fact, it's unlike any of the stores that often surround it in your local mall. From the product displays to the lighting to the sales associates to the cash registers (or lack of), every detail is different, so even when you are just walking by the store catches your attention.

Opening a storefront is not a revolutionary idea. How you open a storefront can be.

Maybe you approach your signage differently. Maybe you have an interesting location. Maybe your staff is unique in their approach or attire. Maybe your store's décor stands out. Maybe you are more exclusive than similar services nearby, or maybe you are less exclusive. Naming an example for each of these stand out points in your area should not be too difficult, and that's the idea. Choosing to compete–from a marketing perspective–at a different point than your competitors does not have to mean inventing an entirely new marketing channel.

Process Overview

For this book, our innovation and iteration process will work through the following stages:

1. **Framework Analysis -** What it means to find a side door and how it could help your business.
2. **Learn from Your Data** - Assess the business intelligence you already have and use it to find insights.
3. **Research Your Market** – Go beyond the knowledge you have to answer important questions about your business, your competitors, and how your target audience thinks.
4. **Brainstorm Templates** – Kickstart your ideation process with some pre-built lens for thinking about innovation.
5. **Evaluate Your Sales Funnel** – With a collection of potential innovation ideas, map out your current business engine and see how the new ideas might fit and what they might impact.
6. **Test Your Innovation** – Build a relatively low-budget version of your innovation to see how your audience responds before investing in a full launch.
7. **Prepare for Launch** – Review your final checklist before hitting the ignition button.
8. **Launch** – Send your new idea into the world.
9. **Learn and Innovate Again** – Use your innovation as a springboard for continued innovation.

Finding the Untapped Node

In our Apple example, they recognized that the majority of their competitors provided an in-person experience via an electronics retailer. In this setting, Apple could not control the presentation or the sales experience. Their products would be on crowded shelves alongside competitor displays, and the long term customer service experience would also be in the hands of a third party as users encountered defects or technical issues.

Apple looked at marketing models that other high-end retailers used, recognized that electronics manufacturers weren't using those models, and applied them to their business. The result is an electronics model with a fashion boutique feel: limited inventory on display (a lot of calculated empty space), modern hipster-chic décor, and sales staff trained exclusively on the products in the store.

Essentially, Apple hijacked a marketing model from another industry, which is one method you can use to find a side door. Don't worry, we are going to look at this

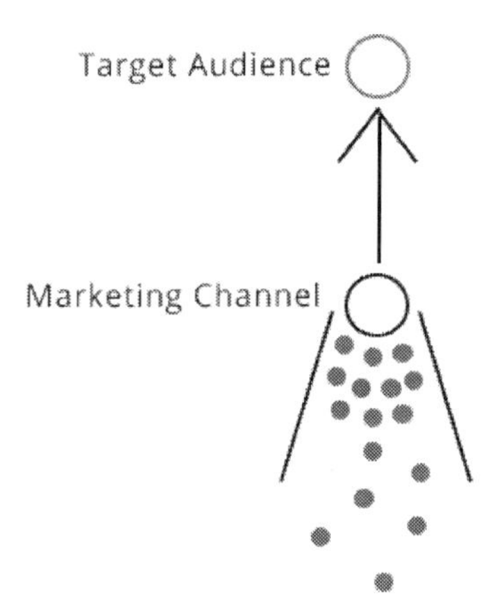

method and many more in greater depth later in this book. For now, however, I want to spend a bit more time on the foundational principles of a niche marketing strategy.

What Apple did with their brick and mortar locations was tap into a different node, or waypoint, that their competitors were not using. We can visualize it like this:

This is why I use the term "node." The marketing channel that we use to reach a target audience is very much a connecting point on a pathway. You go from your business, to the node, and then (hopefully) reach your intended audience. In our

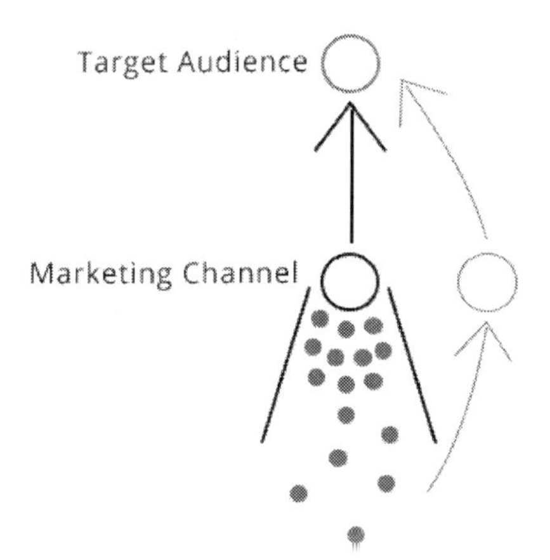

Apple example, the red dots are competing electronics retailers, the black node is the popular marketing channel (third party retailers), and the green node is the highly valued target audience of consumers that want to buy laptops, phones, and mp3 players. The usual route is crowded and extremely competitive. By opening their own brick and mortar locations, Apple used a different node to reach their target audience.

They blazed a path so that they could get to their target audience without having to fight through the noise of every other electronics manufacturer in the market. There are some important takeaways here:

- For this approach to work, your audience must also be somehow connected with your "side door" node. In Apple's case, their target audience shopped at both big box electronics stores and also at malls.
- If the diagram looks like the side path is the long way around, that's because it is. Opening your own store, training your staff, and managing your own distribution–in the case of Apple–is expensive. Blazing a new trail is about being more effective and not necessarily about making your work easier.
- A side door node does not have to be, and in many cases is not, a completely untouched marketing channel. Malls are saturated with retail marketing messages, but Apple put a new spin on it. When you look for your own side door node, don't expect to find some completely virgin marketing soil that has never been touched by another marketer.
- Charting uncharted territory is not without risk. If you try to do something new and untested, there is a chance that the test will fail. Plan accordingly.
- A side door today might not be a side door tomorrow. If you are successful, imitators will follow you down the path you created. If you perform at a high level, you can dominate that route, but you should also be on the lookout for new side doors.

Exceptional marketers have been using this framework for decades, intentionally or intuitively. What we're going to do in this book is you give a process for making this happen in your own business. We will look at a step by step method for finding a side door access point for your target audience and work through a number of examples, big and small, to illustrate the application of the ideas we are covering.

2

FINDING YOUR SIDE DOOR

The call to "be different" or to "be innovative" is frustrating for most business owners. Of course you want to be different. Of course you want to be innovative. But how? You can't just pull a unique idea off of a shelf. You can throw a near infinite amount of time and money at a marketing idea and still fail. If there is a magic switch, even the biggest brands with the biggest budgets haven't been able to find it.

I'm not claiming to have the solution for your business. Even though I've worked with a wide range of clients in a wide range of industries, chances are I don't intuitively understand exactly what you do and exactly what makes you different from your competitors. Instead, we are going to work through a process that I've learned through my work, pulling from my experience with other marketing experts, other marketing agencies, and with business owners. I've spent years testing this approach, and I continue to use it today. Let's get started.

Innovation Starts with Homework

An old adage says that today's leaders are "standing on the shoulders of giants." That's because each generation builds on the advances of the previous generation. The same is true for marketing. You should never start from a blank slate. Instead, you should start with a trove of research and potential points of inspiration. In terms of research, we won't cover anything groundbreaking here, but as fundamental as these suggestions are, many business owners still neglect to adopt them.

If you don't know where you are, deciding how to get where you want to go will be very difficult. But that's enough metaphors and adages. Here are some data points you should explore:

Who are your customers? Why do they do business with you? You can gather this information from your surveys, customer interviews, website analytics, social media analytics, sales data, and also from employee/sales person interviews.

How are customers finding you? Look at your website analytics for search engine data, referral traffic (the sites that customers click from to get to your site) for digital traffic, and consider coupon codes, customer surveys, and customer interviews for your physical traffic.

What do your customers already find engaging about your brand? Use your website analytics to see what pages or blog posts on your site get the most attention and see the longest view times. Go back through your social media channels to see what posts or pieces of content got the most activity from your audience, and talk to your salespeople about the conversation points get them the most traction with prospects.

What are customers saying about you? Set up a Google Alert for key phrases associated with your business, like your brand name and product names. You should also pay attention to social media conversations on and off your social properties, reviews on sites like Yelp and Google Places, and potential news or blog conversations about what you do and your industry in general.

What advertising or marketing initiatives have you used and how did they go? Pull as much information on your previous marketing efforts as you can. Look at everything from impressions (how many people saw the initiative) to conversions (how many people made a purchase as a result of the campaign).

What are your competitors doing and what are their customers saying about them? Being obsessive about monitoring your competitor's movements can eventually become an impediment to progress, but you should still keep a casual eye on their promotions and the new things they might be trying. Get on their email lists and follow their social media at a minimum.

What are interesting brands doing? Innovation in one industry often ripples into other, seemingly unrelated industries. If you make it a point to follow brands known for doing interesting things, you are more likely to be on the edge of what's new and to come up with some interesting ideas along the way. We'll dig into this idea more later.

My framing of these suggestions as questions is deliberate. I often talk to business owners that gather massive amounts of data. They make pie charts and graphs and talk about how this metric changed from month to month, but they often fail to get to anything actionable. The volume of data you have is meaningless if you have no way of making that data meaningful. One of the easiest ways to start finding useful insights from your data is to enter that data with a specific question in mind.

When you approach data with the intention of answering a question, you will get more creative about finding applicable answers in the information in front of you. It takes some practice, and you can find dozens upon dozens of guides online for the most popular platforms (Google Analytics, Facebook Insights, etc.) if you want to really immerse yourself. For our purposes though, the above starting points are good enough.

After you have spent time with your research, answering the sorts of questions I listed above, you can start to look for new marketing opportunities. Again, a heuristic approach is ideal. Looking to answer specific questions is a lot easier than trying to draw unprompted conclusions. Here are some of the questions I use with my clients and with my businesses that you can apply to your own work:

- **Did anything in your research surprise you?** Whenever we identify a data point or a trend or an idea that defies our assumptions, we are likely close to a new opportunity. For example, if you assume that your target demographic is of a certain age and has certain interests, finding that the people actually buying your product are different from your prediction is an exciting prospect. Even if there is only one variable that changes–like age–you could be on the verge of accidently unlocking a new market.
- **Can you identify any trends?** Data tells a story. If you look at your data overtime, you should be able to get a sense for the direction your business or industry as a whole is moving. Perhaps customers are buying more of one product and less of another. Perhaps customers are buying more at a certain time of year. Perhaps one location is outperforming another location. Perhaps your industry is starting to adopt new technology or new processes. Keeping a finger on the pulse of what's going on can help you to be proactive rather than reactive.

- **Who do you share your customers with?** The modern consumer is bombarded by advertisements and offers in all aspects of their life, personal and professional. If you take the time to define and understand the people buying your products, you should be able to step into their shoes and identify other brands–not necessarily competitors–that are targeting the same consumers. Start paying attention to what they're doing!
- **What messages or touchpoints are stickiest?** If you are remotely active on social media, with a blog, or with some form of advertising, you can use your analytics to identify the messages or efforts that your audience finds more engaging. Knowing what is working–and what is not working–is critical to informing your future marketing decisions.
- **Of what customers are saying, what stands out to you?** Just as we did in the research, when we look at customer feedback and sort through interview transcripts, anything that surprises you has potential value. That means you had an assumption that might not be accurate or you uncovered an angle or path that you were unaware of. These are both big opportunities.
- **What are customers saying about your competitors?** Thanks to social media and the expanse of the web, finding out how customers feel about the competition is not all that hard to do. If you look at the types of comments they receive and reviews they accumulate, you can get a sense of where customers are getting frustrated in the market. That could end up being an opportunity to you.

To be fair, there is a near infinite depth that you can take with your research analysis. Entire departments and companies are built around this very task, but our goal is to be more strategic. We're thinking big picture. If you walk away from this process with two or three potential insights to explore, you are in good shape. All you really need is one, but having a few that you can discard gives you a bit more freedom and takes off a lot of the pressure.

These insights will become the leveraging factors that allows you to tap into a side door node. They become the initial opportunities for diverting users away from the primary marketing path that they usually take. If you can't uncover something new or untapped about your audience or the way they view your industry, all is not lost. We can work backward from the end point, which we will talk about later, but you will still need to confirm in some way that your audience will have a reason to want to use the new path you create.

In Apple's case, their research might have found that their savviest, most passionate users were early adopters in more than one regard, not just tech. They think of themselves as being trendy, as using the best, and as being different. If those same high-end electronics users are likely to shop at a high-end fashion boutique, then maybe we're on to something. Maybe we could learn from that model and apply it to new a space because now we have some evidence to support that the idea could actually work.

If you cringed on the word "maybe," good. This is not foolproof, and you should know that going in. Before we invest a massive amount of budget in a hunch, we will test our side door node to make sure that it actually excites our audience that we think it will.

Before that though, we need to identify a node for us to test.

Node Templates

Earlier in the book, I said that our goal with this process is not to reinvent the wheel. The chances of our uncovering some entirely new completely untouched marketing opportunity are absurdly small. Instead, we can learn from how the pieces on the board have been used already–by us, by our competitors, and by companies in completely different industries–and find new ways to use those pieces.

In my creative work, I have identified five fundamental templates that you can use to kick start your ideation process. Your final side door node might borrow from a few of these categories or not quite comfortably into any category in particular, but that's okay. Remember that our goal is to give you a framework for discovery, for moving through data and asking yourself "What if we..." until your own answer to that question knocks your socks off.

For each of the five templates I cover here, I will briefly summarize a case study example of this marketing strategy in a real world business. My hope is that seeing the template in action will help you to understand the mechanics at work and to see how you might apply it to your own business.

1. Hijack a Model

Transplant an approach or business model from a seemingly unrelated industry and apply it to your own.

We informally explored this example in our earlier discussion of Apple stores, but let's start from the beginning for the sake of clarity. In this template, you look at what a successful business in another industry does well and challenge yourself to think about how you could do something similar in your own business.

- What if we designed our store to look like a store from this other kind of business?
- What if we did events like this other business?
- What if we made ads inspired by this other business?
- If we took a sales person from this space and asked him to sell our product, what would be different?
- What if we targeted the same audience as this other business?
- What if we were in a similar location as this other business?

Some of the answers to these questions will feel silly, but don't let that deter you from continuing to think on them. What if your hardware store was more like a skate shop? What does that even mean? Well, a skate shop usually tries to be a bit more upbeat than a hardware store. Skate shops put it a bit more effort into the aesthetics of the shop experience, and they go out of their way to show how connected they are to the local skate community, often decorating the store with pictures big and small of local skaters doing something cool in local skate shops. Also, skate shops tend to be staffed by passionate experts, the kind of people that make sure you have the best and most appropriate set up.

If a hardware store had to function more like a skate shop, what would need to change? Well, hardware stores tend to be staffed by experts, but are they passionate and engaging? That's a potential opportunity. The aesthetics of the average hardware store are pretty plain. It's hardly a destination. That's a potential opportunity. What if part of the new store look was featuring pictures from around the community of local carpenters, handymen, and painters in action or at the very least their completed projects?

It might not be the right answer yet, but we now have a series of possibilities that are radically different from what our competitors are doing in their stores because none of our competitors are doing the mental exercise of imagining their business as being something so different.

Case Study: Steam becomes the iTunes of video games

Apple's launch of iTunes revolutionized the way we distribute, experience, and market music. By creating a way to easily access music digitally, Apple gave their target audiences a reason to return repeatedly to a platform that they could control and grow, all while collecting insightful data and direct user feedback. At this point, we take this move for granted, but at the time, iTunes was a major disruption in the music industry.

Valve started as a company that made video games. The first Half-Life shattered records, won a mountain of awards, and set new standards for the first person shooter video game genre. They saw continued success when they took the fan-made Counter Strike and gave it an official release. Eventually, Valve saw an opportunity in digital distribution. When they first launched Steam, they seemed to use it primarily for copyright protection. By forcing users to install Steam when they purchased Half-Life 2, they could verify that users were in fact playing the game from a legitimate copy.

But then Valve started to offer downloads and purchases through Steam. And then third party developers started to sell their games through Steam. The platform has seen dozens of iterations, both big and small, over the years. In 2015, SteamSpy estimated that Valve generated upward of $3.5 billion from their platform.

Now, I don't have a source that says "Valve's leadership looked directly at iTunes and decided to do exactly that" but by us simply being able to say "This thing is a lot like this thing, except they are in two very different industries" we can clearly see the value of this line of thinking.

2. Befriend the Gatekeeper

Identify a non-competitor that has already captured the audience you want and work through them.

What we are essentially talking about here are finding partnerships, but the way most people think of partnerships is far too limiting for our purposes. A productive partnership is not simply a handshake agreement that says "hey, let's send each other referrals." An effective partnership is much more creative and far more structured, creating a dynamic where both parties benefit.

- What businesses or organizations already have access to the audience you want?
- Are they working with any other partners currently? If so, what are they doing?
- How can your business compliment or further the goals of this other business?
- What do you already have in common with this business or organization?
- Have any of your competitors attempted partnerships? What did they do and how did it work?
- Is there a cause or community group that your audience/employees has a vested interest in?

When we first mapped out how the usual marketing path creates a bottleneck of competition, I said that established brands are difficult to unseat because they have achieved a great amount of control over their own access to a desired audience. For this template, we are taking a "don't beat them; join them!" approach to solving our problem of connecting with a target audience.

How these partnerships can actually play out is worthy of a book in its own right, but the characteristics of a good partnership tend to stem from one key idea: both parties come out ahead. Getting to this result can play out in many ways. Maybe a business helps a non-profit raise money (corporate social responsibility; a worthwhile topic to explore separately from our work here). Maybe two businesses come together to market a dual service. Maybe two businesses come together to make a new product. Maybe two businesses agree to combine marketing budgets to target the same audience. Or maybe one business licenses the brand recognition from another business.

There are some great examples of each of these avenues. A slew of businesses work with non-profits to varying degrees. Mortgage brokers and realtors often combine forces to simplify the home buying process. Taco Bell and Doritos spent months perfecting the Doritos Locos Taco. Financial advisors often partner with CPAs to deliver seminars or to better serve clients. Happy Feet, of Shark Tank fame, licensed DreamWorks characters for their slippers, giving them an edge in competing for store space and for attracting new customers.

The right partnership can be a complete game-changer.

Case Study: Sarris Candies builds a community army

Frank Sarris founded Sarris Candies in his basement but by 1963 had grown to the point that he could open his own shop. Today, Sarris Candies is something of a chocolate goliath in the greater Pittsburgh region, and their growth continues. According to Smart Business, Sarris Candies is a $45 million company that employs over 500 people, which isn't bad for a company that started with one person in his basement.

While a number of factors have contributed to the success of Sarris Candies, like the quality of their products and how they treat their employees, one facet stuck out to Bill Sarris (Frank's son) when I interviewed him for a podcast.

Fundraising.

When Bill was in high school, he was class president, and they needed to raise $2000. He designed a program where his classmates could sell his dad's candy in exchange for a piece of the profit, and the class raised $8000. The success of that small pilot program turned a light on for the Sarris family. They realized that they could simultaneously support their local communities and leverage an army of young, energetic salespeople.

This angle helped to set Sarris Candies apart from what was actually a competitive candy market at the time, and fundraising is still an important part of their revenue model. Today, thanks to fundraising, they have dozens of community partners–schools, sports teams, nonprofit organizations, and so on---championing the Sarris brand. While we might not think of the fundraising model as revolutionary today, there are plenty of creative ways that your business can piggyback on a good cause to both promote positive change and to grow your business. Sarris Candies is a great example of how that initiative can become a core part of your brand identity.

3. Change the Timing

Identify the standard cadence of your industry and set your business to a different beat.

Rhythm is a fairly abstract idea to discuss in isolation, but most industries follow some sort of yearly pattern. There are slow days and busy days, slow seasons and busy seasons. There might be that one big convention every year. There might be a time of year where everyone announces their new products. And then there are the classic holiday marketing periods. If you disconnect your marketing from this usual schedule–even if it's only at one point–the customers that have been trained to follow the same cadence are likely to notice.

- Can you deliver your ads at a different time or place?
- Can you deliver your products or services faster?
- Can you use a slowdown in your business model to create the feeling of exclusivity or rarity?
- Can you deliver faster customer service?
- Can you buck the trend of a standard industry schedule?
- Can you make your customer a more involved participant in the process?

As we've discussed many times before, our goal is not necessarily to invent an entirely new piece of marketing strategy. If we can set ourselves apart, even in a small way, at one or more critical points, we can effectively get to our target audience through a side door node. The timing of your marketing efforts alone could be enough to set you apart.

When I talk with clients about timing, usually the conversation immediately becomes about how a business can be faster or how a business can get somewhere before the competition. Speed can definitely be a part of the marketing here, and businesses like Amazon and McDonald's have demonstrated that it can be effective, but it can also be an expensive race that you don't ever want to enter.

Instead, timing could actually be about slowing some parts of your business down. Many clubs and restaurants make you wait to enter or to get a table out of a combination of necessity and also exclusivity. Chipotle and Subway take what used to be a simple process–ordering a sandwich or a burrito–and expand the experience into stages so that customers have a greater input into the experience.

If you assemble a collection of the schedules, processes, and calendars related to your business, you can start to imagine how your business might change if you shifted a schedule earlier or later, made it shorter or longer, or transplanted one piece and put it somewhere completely new. The opportunities that come out of it might surprise you.

Case Study: Sega cuts to the front of the retailer line

For a long time, the electronics world has been dominated by a few key tradeshows, with the Electronics Entertainment Expo (E3) reigning as king until recently. In the early 90s, when Nintendo dominated the home video game market and the scrappy upstart Sega was fighting for a piece of the pie, E3 became a battleground. Nintendo and Sega would try to outdo each other in every way.

Bigger announcements. Bigger booths. Bigger parties. Bigger demos.

It was an arms race, and Nintendo had the upper hand. Nintendo controlled most of the market, and they had a far larger budget. The marketing team at Sega, at an especially pivotal point in the company's career, realized that they couldn't risk pitting their next big announcement directly against Nintendo's (unknown) next big announcement. Nintendo's advantage was simply too great.

So rather than waiting for E3, Sega held its own event. They invited representatives from retailers across the country to Florida for an exclusive look at the future of Sega. And they did it weeks before E3. While Nintendo was still waiting to announce their play, Sega executives hob-knobbed with the key leaders they needed to get their products in more stores around the country. They did it at their own conference where they could control almost every element.

The play gave Sega a valuable foothold in the market, helping to make Sega a household name in the video game console world. Though Nintendo and Sega have both fallen from grace in recent times, they were giants in this era. For Sega, the rise to giant-hood was possible in part because they refused to compete on the same schedule as Nintendo.

4. Throw Out the Standards

Deliberately ignore the standard conventions of an advertising channel or platform.

One of the most memorable figures from anyone's childhood is the class clown. We are less likely to remember the classmates who turned their homework in on time, never spoke out of turn, and stayed within the lines. Yes, rules are made to be obeyed, but we also tend to notice and remember the rule-breakers far more often than the rule-keepers. If you can identify the rules that govern a marketing channel or vehicle and then strategically break them, by virtue of simply breaking a rule your message is likely to garner more attention.

- What are the best practices of this marketing channel? Does any particular variable seem arbitrary?
- If the channel is visual, can you do more or less than the norm?
- Also if the channel is visual, can you literally work outside of the box in terms of dimensions and creative material?
- Pick a marketing vehicle. What would the "anti" version of that vehicle look like?
- What is the current trend in each channel? How can you buck that trend?

To be clear, this template is not about doing anything illegal. The rules I'm talking about fall more into the category of "This is always how we've done it." If you can find a point in a marketing channel where someone says that sentence, you probably have an opportunity to do something new. This might not sound like you are blazing a new trail, but it can elevate you beyond the standard competitive points.

For example, billboards are a well-defined canvas. The sign is this big, so your image must also be this big. For some time, the fight for attention in billboard advertising was a mix of picking the right location and making the best rectangular ad. Everyone was making the same shaped ads. But what if the cowboy on our billboard has his hat poking up over the billboard? Well, now the shape of the box has changed, making this one billboard stand out more than the others.

It's not a complicated paradigm shift, but the change is large enough that consumers notice. The rule was that billboard ads had to be rectangles, but did they really? Apparently not.

You don't have to be beholden to the rules of the market or the industry–in a marketing sense; not a legal and ethical sense. If you can step outside the norm, in even a seemingly small way, consumers will take notice. That doesn't mean that your entire business has to be built off the grid, but a few well-placed marketing efforts can separate you from the pack.

Case Study: Sears rises to the top of the stack

The Sears of yesteryear was a retail goliath that reached beyond the Sears stores we know today and into credit card processing as well as insurance. At its start in 1893, Sears was selling watches and soon entered the highly competitive direct mail catalog game.

This was a bold move for Sears. The established name at the time was Montgomery Ward, and they had been selling to customers through catalogs for 20 years. By 1900, however, Sears overtook Montgomery Ward, racking up $11 million in sale, which is an incredible profit for a young company even without adjusting for inflation.

To make the Sears catalog stand out, Richard Sears built on a keen observation: homeowners often stacked their magazines and books from biggest to smallest, and those piles of periodicals often included the very mail order catalogs Sears was aiming to compete against. To ensure that the Sears catalog would be at the top of the stack–and in effect, top of mind for consumers–Sears printed their catalogs in dimensions smaller than the standard.

In print, usually a conversation is about more, especially when product photos and flavor copy are in the mix. If the catalog is bigger, surely we can make the sales pitches inside more vibrant and more engaging, but instead Sears saw that actually going smaller was the answer by virtue of simply how consumers would interact with the catalog itself.

The catalog alone was not a silver bullet for Sears. The company made a lot of shrewd and clever business decisions that built and accelerated its momentum, and the catalog is once piece of that bigger picture. At the same time, however, this classic example perfectly illustrates the return you can get from strategically breaking a rule.

5. Think Big About Going Small

Narrow your audience to an incredibly small and specific slice.

I know, I know. Every marketing guide ever will tell you that you should narrow your audience to a group of people most relevant to your niche. The advice is still good, but few businesses are following it. For the businesses that do follow it, many of them continue to overlook opportunities to make their marketing unique because they are simply marketing too broadly. Now, perhaps more than ever, we have the tools to make personal touches in marketing more efficient and more effective, but many brands are still not inclined to zoom-in on more specific opportunities.

- Can you offer more personalized, one-on-one customer service?
- Can the targeting and messaging of your ads be more specific?
- Can you incorporate more direct interaction with your prospects?
- Can you leverage variations in geography?
- Can you incorporate some degree of exclusivity into your campaign?

Most brands want to be as big as possible, so when they look to expand their audience, they often try to hit as many people as possible with a given campaign. Even the narrower campaigns are still incredibly broad in terms of the conversation we are having here.

A Super Bowl ad is easily one of the broadest ad efforts possible. Yes, most viewers are vaguely interested in football fans, but beyond that there are few unifying demographic details that makes the audience in anyway homogenous. The range of ages, locations, income levels, interests, and beliefs is so wildly diverse that even the "greatest Super Bowl ads" give up on really communicating about the product or brand. When brands thing about making a big splash, they usually think that means reaching as many people as people–the Super Bowl mindset.

Flip the script. You can make a bigger splash by narrowing the experience. Think about it: the public doesn't react to John Cena hanging out at a baseball game nearly as much as it does when John Cena–the professional wrestler and actor–visits a child cancer patient. The individual faces make the story compelling. It's something real to latch on to and gives the brand something concrete to echo off of. Think about what hospital visits say about John Cena versus what a Budweiser ad with horses and puppies says about the beer. One has far more substance than the other, as I'm sure you'll agree.

Case Study: The PT Services Group

The PT Services Group connects insurance and financial advisors to new business opportunities. They reach out to potential prospects on an advisor's behalf, build interest, and set the first appointment. From there, the advisor takes over, stepping into the first meeting to begin the sales process. For the advisor, this means skipping the difficult and time-consuming research and cold calling process.

PT–who is a client of mine, by the way–has done this for over 20 years, and has it down to a science. They know that 50 calling hours, working through some 2000 (or more) prospects in a driving radius of up to 60 minutes, results in an average of four to six appointments. That might sound like a small return, but these are high-value prospects. Closing just one of these sales can mean a record-breaking year for the advisor.

As part of a new pilot program, they partnered with an industry thought leader, Charlie Epstein of 401k Coach, to send 200 prospects a copy of his book, Paychecks for Life, on the advisor's behalf. In this new model, prospects get a book from the advisor in the mail–a nice, thought-provoking gift–and the PT team of sales associates followed up later with their tried-and-true approach to appointment setting.

For the same 50 hours of calling, PT set eight appointments. That's double the return, and the only thing that changed was the addition of a free book. According to Epstein, the assumption is that sending someone a book triggers a need to reciprocate in some way. You gave someone a book, and they automatically feel more inclined–obligated even–to talk with you.

A traditional mindset might tell you to cast a wider net, but if you do more for the audience you're trying to reach your message might actually be more impactful.

3

PICKING YOUR PATH

Being an innovative brand does not mean that you have to innovate every possible turn or that you have to abandon traditional marketing practices. Finding the right place to innovate is just as important as the innovation itself. If you've been following along, you should have a whiteboard or notebook full of potential niche marketing ideas by now. You should have identified some side door nodes that might make sense to your business and put some tentative thought into how you could leverage them.

Before you commit to a new marketing initiative, we should take a closer look at what you're doing now and how well it's working.

Ideally, your innovation should make sense in the broader context of your other marketing tactics. It doesn't make sense to have an innovative ad campaign, for example, if you don't have the website or sales process to support it. As we map out the components of your new business engine, keep these points in mind:

1. A powerful innovation could correct a weakness in your current marketing mix.
2. It could also augment an existing strength, helping you to dig your heels into an advantage you've already claimed.
3. Adopting an innovation might mean tweaking or adjusting other facets of your marketing.

The Mapping Process

When I sit down with a new client, I start with a fundamental question: how does your business grow?

The question is surprisingly difficult. The knee-jerk response is to say, "By making sales," but that's the what, not the how. What this question aims to uncover is the engine that moves a business forward. What parts do what? How does one part need to perform for the others to also perform at their best? How do they connect? What makes this engine more effective than the engines our competitors are using?

In businesses big and small, I've found that clients consistently struggle to explain the marketing mechanisms that actually move them closer to their goals.

Not long ago, I was working with a technology company. Their marketing team wanted to use a combination of blog content and email marketing to generate and nurture leads. This is fairly standard as far as content marketing goes, but for us to close more sales, we needed to know what the sales team did with the leads. In the salespeople's minds, what should a prospect learn from our content and from our email marketing? What does an ideal prospect look like and what are some of the common challenges they face in early conversations? What does the sales process look like?

The marketing team didn't know, and they hadn't asked.

If we had moved forward with any sort of new initiative–let alone something bold and innovative–without looking at the bigger picture, we might have been able to generate a mountain of new leads, but that wouldn't matter if they weren't the leads the sales team needed.

This happens often. Fixating on the one specific result you want to drive–leads, web traffic, Facebook likes–can blind you to what you should really be trying to accomplish: making the entire car go faster rather than just polishing one specific part. This is why you need to map the entirety of your new business engine. For your marketing to be efficient and effective, you need to understand every part of your new business engine. You need to map your funnel.

The Sales Funnel Process

Turning your marketing strategy into a cohesive collection of marketing tactics is a big challenge that many business owners struggle to overcome. There are so many different avenues that your business could potentially explore or are currently using that it's easy to lose track of what one vehicle should be doing and how it should be

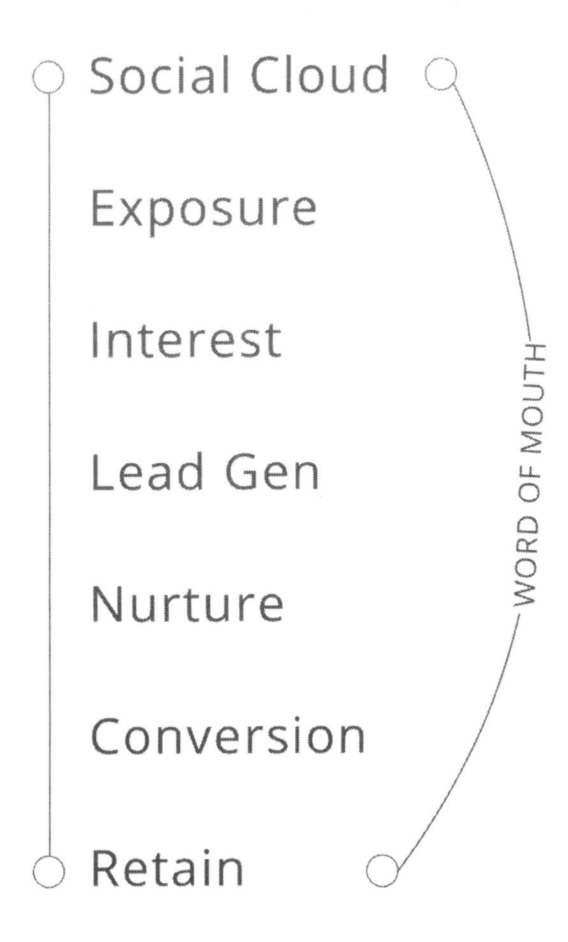

supporting the rest of your plan. This sales funnel exercise helps you to zoom out and look at the entire engine all at once.

I say sales funnel because that makes the most sense to me in my own mind. You might call it a marketing map or a buyer's journey or a magical bread crumb trail. The goal is to take an inventory of every piece you have on the board and identify the job it does in your marketing mix. From there, you can more effectively identify weaknesses in your marketing engine and measure your efforts because you can say:

- This tactic's job is to do X.

- We can know this tactic is effective when it does X.
- This tactic is designed to connect with tactic Y.

With this framework, you can understand what bucket a particular tactic fits into and what that bucket as a whole is trying to accomplish for your brand. Keep in mind that this is general. Every business is different, so while a sales funnel represents the fundamental way most businesses operate, there might be a nuance to your business that changes this model somewhat. Also keep in mind that one tactic could serve multiple purposes. That's okay. From here, we will walk through each stage of the sales funnel, discuss what tactics might fit into that stage, and give you some insight into how to be effective both at that stage and in moving to the next.

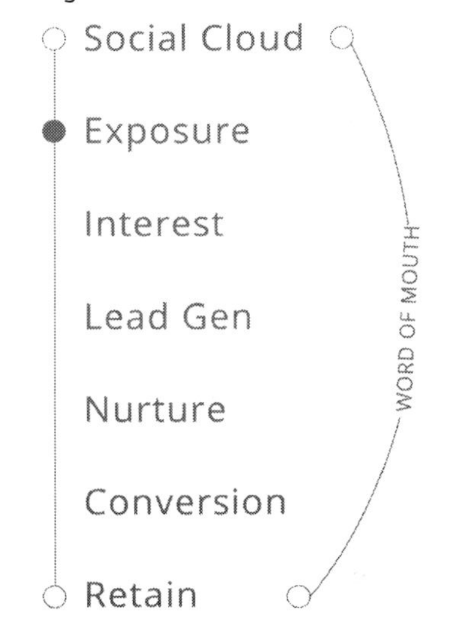

Exposure

This is the stage where a potential customer first learns about your business. Exposure is critical, but many business owners and advertising agencies use the idea of exposure as a catch-all. Yes, you need exposure to eventually generate sales, but as you can see by looking at the funnel, exposure is pretty far away from conversion. Equating exposure with business growth is a big mistake. Turning exposure into revenue takes work. The exposure stage usually occurs prior to prospects visiting your website or stopping by your store. You might generate exposure through:

- Advertisements
- Signage
- Events
- Flyers
- A shared content (a social post or a blog post for example)
- News coverage of your business
- Networking
- Direct mail

- Word of mouth (more on that later)
- Search engine
- Conference booth
- Some other discovery engine like Yelp

This is not a definitive list. These are just some of the more typical tactics, and in all cases their job is to drive relevant traffic to a place where those prospects can start to learn more about who you are and what you do. Businesses are always finding creative ways to build awareness for what they do, and I encourage you to be as original as possible on this front because the more of the right people you get into the funnel the more sales you will ultimately generate. Once you get the attention of your target audience, you have to keep it.

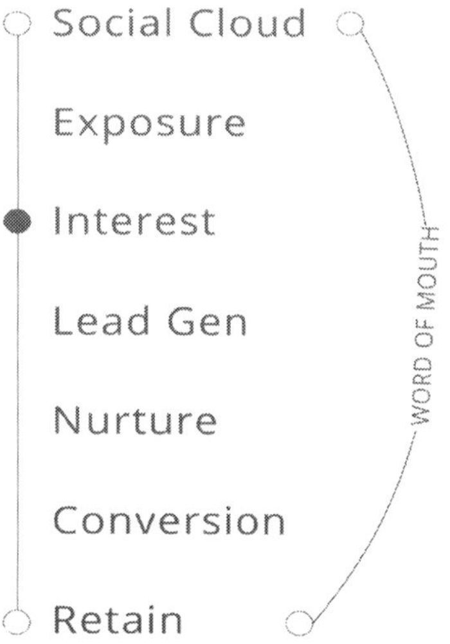

Social Cloud
Exposure
Interest
Lead Gen
Nurture
Conversion
Retain
WORD OF MOUTH

Interest-Building

So a customer hears about your business. What next? If the exposure vehicle did its job, then the exposure should have driven the prospect to a platform of some sort. Usually, this is your website, but it could also be your physical location if you are running a brick & mortar business. If you are running a brick & mortar business, it could be conceivably both. The prospect should land somewhere where you control the narrative so that you can craft a message and an experience that makes the customer more interested in what you do.

Typically, your website will do a lot of the heavy lifting here, but other vehicles can help to educate a prospect about what makes your business worth caring about and your products worth learning about. At this stage, you might use some combination of the following:

- Website
- Sales rep (at a store, at a conference)
- Customer testimonials

- Case studies
- Educational videos
- Blog content
- Re-targeting ads

The potential for combination is important to note here. Building interest also means building trust, so one website visit might not do the trick, especially if the jump from prospect to customer is a pricey one. This is normal, and it's a challenge you should account for. If you account for it properly, your interest-building will generate leads.

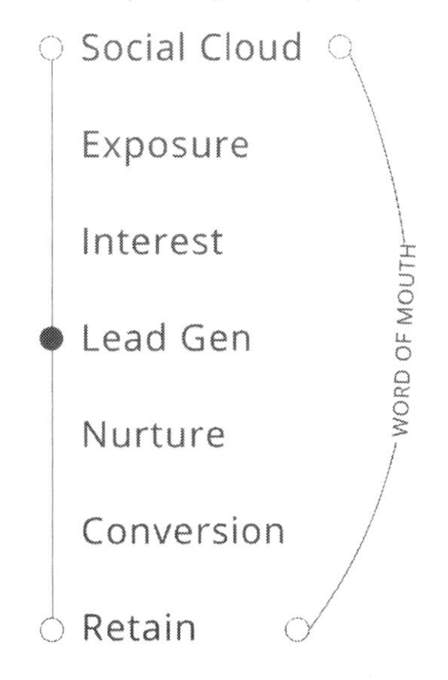

Lead Generation

Lead generation is anything that gets a prospect to opt-in to more direct communication. If you get a name, an email, and/or a phone number, you now have a lead. Once you get a lead, you have permission to speak directly to someone that has at least some interest in what you have to offer. If they didn't, why would they give you your information? The role that leads play in your sales process might vary a bit, but they matter for pretty much everyone. For someone selling a big ticket item to other business owners, there could be a few months between lead generation and the final sale.

If you are a more consumer-focused retailer, you might generate the lead immediately prior to the sale or even during the sale (at which point the information becomes a retention tool). It will never be a bad thing to capture prospect information, ever, so it should be a part of your sales funnel. In short, you typically offer a giveaway or a "magnet" to motivate someone to fork over some contact info. These are some of the commons lead magnets:

- White paper
- E-book
- Coupon

- Sneak peek
- Free trial

The beauty of the sales funnel is that you can measure every tactic you can choose to incorporate. A breakdown in the lead generation stage should be a trigger to reevaluate all of the stages that proceed it. If you are generating traffic but not generating leads, you are probably not generating the right kind of traffic and need to revise your exposure and interest-building vehicles. If you are sure that you are generating the right traffic, then it's likely that your lead magnet is simply not enticing enough. Think of ways that you can add more value to your prospect's life so that you can move forward into warming more leads.

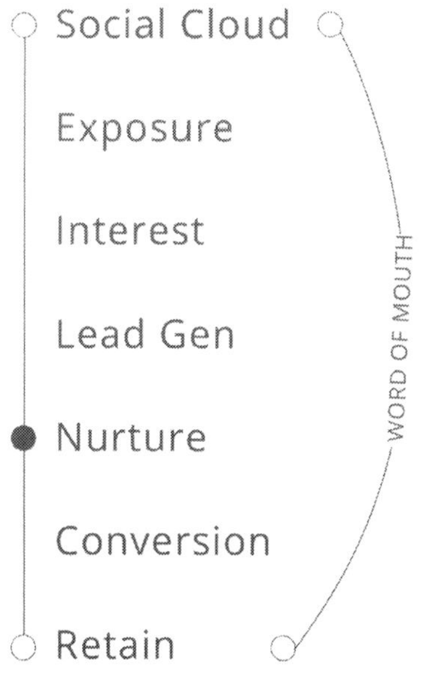

Lead Nurturing

Your customer opted in for more communication from you, so now you follow-up directly to continue building the relationship. There is some sales-pitching going on here, but this stage is just as much about creating trust and providing value. The exact angle you take will depend on your industry and your target audience, but the typical approach is to get the lead and follow up with an automated email campaign that was pre-built and pre-scheduled. If you are selling a bigger ticket item, likely in the B2B space, your lead nurture process is more likely to mix email with a personal follow-up from a sales person. But there are other options:

- Email
- Sales follow-up (call or email)
- Direct mail
- Re-targeting ads
- Encouragement from existing customers

Lead nurturing is a special art, and it can sometimes take a good bit of time. Slow dripping emails out over a few years is not uncommon for virtually every industry at this point. Sell shoes? Send them an email every week. Want to sell a car? Send them an email every month. That exact interval might not be the magic number for you, but that general principle is consistent. If it's appropriate, that email campaign is augmented through other means, like the occasional phone call or maybe an ad targeted exactly at people who are almost to the point of buying but just need a little itty bit more convincing.

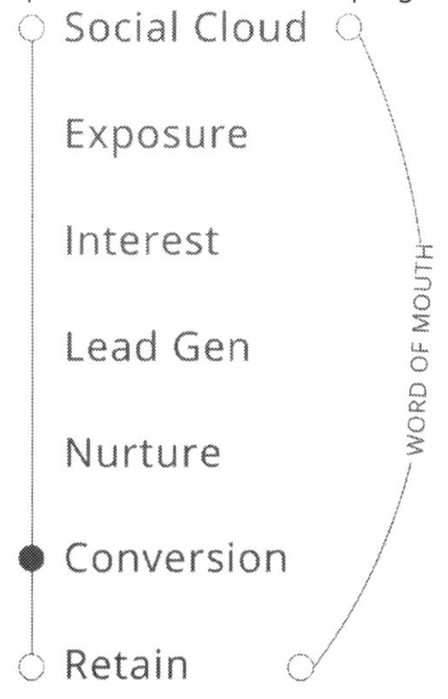

Conversion

The customer buys. This might sound like the simplest part of your sales funnel, but there are still opportunities here to improve the experience and to increase efficiency because our sales funnel does not end at the sale. E-commerce businesses learned a long time ago that every click matters, so even if a prospect is perfectly ready to buy, a wonky purchasing process can either kill the sale or start your customer relationship off on the wrong foot–yeah, they bought your thing but it was kind of miserable to do so. This puts you behind the curve, leaving you to play catch-up, which is not a good place for you to be.

You want your buying experience to be so painless that the customer either doesn't notice it all or is astounded by how special you made them feel. As you work through this stage, you should probably consider:

- E-commerce website
- Point-of-sale (POS) system
- Payment processor
- Sales rep
- Cashier

Many retailers invest a huge amount of resources into optimizing this stage. They test different copy and button colors over and over to get the perfect, highest performing buy page possible. This philosophy can be applied to the process your sales team uses or to how you layout your store. If you knock it out of the park at this stage, you position yourself to improve retention and to drive word of mouth.

Retention

What happens after the purchase could be more lucrative than the purchase itself. That might sound counterintuitive, but Harvard Business Review found that a 5% increase in retention can lead to an 80% increase in profits in some cases. If you follow my work, you'll have heard me cite this statistic before. I harp on it a lot for two reasons: the profit opportunity is huge, and many businesses are so worried about getting people in the front door that they forget to keep them from leaving through the backdoor.

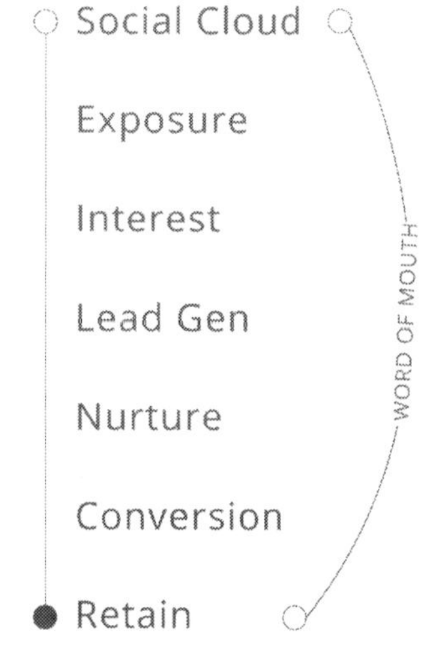

Keeping existing cust-omers is far cheaper than finding new ones, and happy loyal customers are powerful advocates to have on your side. Retaining customers is partially customer service, but it's also very much related to how you maintain genuine, authentic relationships with them in between purchases. If you aren't sure where to start with our own sales funnel, consider starting with this stage. Here are some retention tactics that you might use:

- Customer service
- Email
- Phone calls
- Direct mail (thank you cards, for example)
- Social media
- Blog content
- Customer loyalty programs

Depending on your business, retention could be a challenge to measure, but it's an essential piece of a powerful marketing engine. If your retention efforts are on target, every drop of traffic that enters your sales funnel will become more profitable over the life of your business. Happy customers not only spend more, they tell their friends and colleagues about you as well.

Word of Mouth

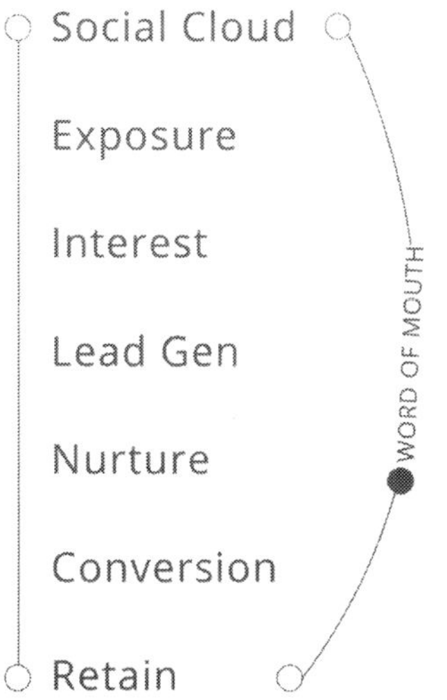

Social Cloud
Exposure
Interest
Lead Gen
Nurture
Conversion
Retain
WORD OF MOUTH

Regardless of the strength of your retention efforts, your customers are likely to talk about your business. The worst case scenario is for your customers to talk negatively about their experience, but it's also dangerous if they flat out don't talk at all. One of the biggest opportunities in our connected world is to have customers promote our businesses on our behalves. If they had good experiences, they'll say something. If they had bad experiences, they'll say something. The goal is to have them be so excited about what you did for them that they shout from the rooftops for you, spreading your brand to their friends and family. Word of mouth is one of the most abstract components of a sales funnel because it can be difficult to track and even harder to stimulate. Difficult doesn't mean impossible, however. Your plan should account for it and incorporate some of the following tactics:

- Social media
- Branded merchandise
- Social media monitoring
- Keyword monitoring
- Sentiment analysis
- Shareable content
- Affiliate marketing
- Review sites and listings
- Thought leader relationships
- Sponsored or paid advocates

Remember, our customers are more connected than ever, and they are more likely to take their complaints to Twitter than they are to take them to your doorstep. If you can leverage that interconnectedness, you can build a largely self-powered sales funnel. And then when you add more exposure tactics to that momentum, your growth can become exponential.

Social Cloud

The word of mouth your customers generate feeds into the social cloud. This is a term I've borrowed from Scott Straaten of Un-Marketing. The social cloud is a quick way of describing all of the possible places where people could be having conversations about or related to your business. This includes online as well as in person, so you need to account for the full spectrum to be effective. The list for this stage can be as long as the world is big, but here are some starting points:

- Social media
- Online forums
- Blogs
- Professional groups
- Hobby groups
- Family gatherings
- Local Publications
- Professional Publications

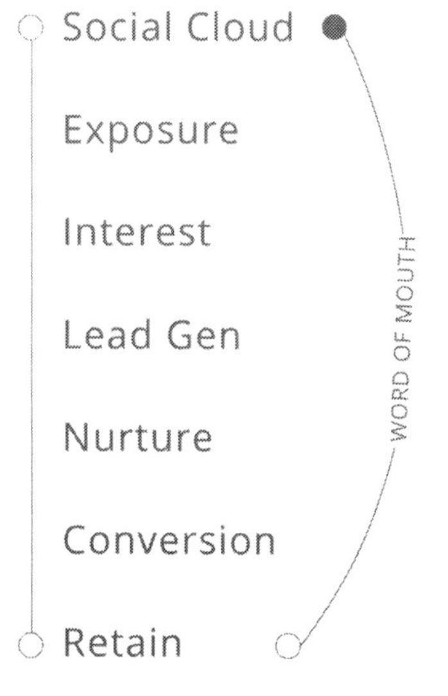

Where your customers and prospects will congregate can vary wildly from industry to industry, but it's still important for you to know where those conversations happen so that you can pay attention to them and also participate in them. If you do your research, you might discover that something as unusual a church group could become a part of your marketing strategy. To really stay on top of these conversations, especially as your brand grows, you should consider using tools like Google Alerts, Hoot Suite, or something as powerful as a sentiment analysis tool like Brandwatch.

Examples

As I've said before, the exact sales funnel you develop will be unique to your business.

The model we just explored is a framework that helps you build and evaluate your own new business engine. Admittedly, the majority of this e-book has been abstract. To make it a bit more concrete, let's work some examples.

Online Children's Clothing Retailer

This brand sells clothing for toddlers, targeting mostly moms on the west coast with a hippy chic practical feminist message–gender equality is powerful but we should also celebrate what makes girls different. The founder quit her job as a high-powered fashion designer to build the business. The sales funnel for this business might look like this:

Exposure – Facebook ads, Pinterest activity, Instagram activity, blogger outreach, and an active public relations effort to the tell the founder's story of leaving the international fashion world behind.

Interest-building – Website, press kit, videos.

Lead generation – A free e-book that features fun and accessible mother-daughter recipe and craft ideas.

Lead nurturing – Emails directly from the founder about the brand's values and the brand's products.

Conversion – A Shopify store with free shipping incentives and vintage, handcrafted tags and packaging that big brands would struggle to emulate.

Retention – Follow-up emails about the brand, its values, and new products.

Word of mouth – Social media and blog content that is colorful, interesting, and highly shareable.

Social cloud – Founder plays an active role in local parent groups, routinely reads and interacts with mommy bloggers as well as other parent-focused online forums.

The advantage of running an e-commerce state is that there is no shortage of data since virtually every touchpoint is digital. This brand could use Facebook conversion pixels and Google Analytics goal-tracking to paint a vivid picture of how prospects are moving through the funnel and interacting with each stage, making it much easier to identify breakdowns in the engine as well as opportunities that warrant additional investment.

Business Consulting Firm

This brand helps business owners increase the efficiency of their internal processes. Unlike the previous example that targeted consumers, this business targets other businesses with a message of rethinking how a business should operate and grow so that it can capture new opportunities and generate more revenue. While the return is potentially significant for a client, the upfront investment is at minimum $15,000 to $30,000. As a result, small business owner prospects are naturally hesitant to make a quick purchasing decisions.

Exposure – Webinars, conference and tradeshow visits, partnerships with professional organizations, thought leadership content on industry websites

Interest-building – Website, customer testimonials, case studies, archive of thought leadership content

Lead generation – Various white papers on industry challenges, webinar registration, contact form

Lead nurturing – Call from a member of the sales team, email campaign about industry challenges and insights, LinkedIn connection

Conversion – Signed contract, access to online payment portal

Retention – Onboarding and training process, actual consulting efforts, communication between client and consultant, continued email follow-up with thought leadership on industry issues, reports on the progress of active projects

Word of mouth – Request for testimonials and case study development, referral fee offer

Social cloud – Active in industry organizations both on and offline, active LinkedIn presence as a company and for individual consultants, engagement with top industry publications and leaders.

The advantage of a business like this is that the higher cost of being a customer naturally leads to more personal attention for the prospect, which is difficult for an online retailer selling t-shirts for $20 each to provide. However, that personal touch is also difficult to track and measure. A sales call won't produce a ream of concrete specific data like a website visit will, but if the sales team has an intuitive customer management system (CMS) and is diligent about taking notes, the business should be able to track where prospects originate and how they move through the funnel.

For example, the business could set up a specific landing page for the next big conference that includes some information about the company and an offer to download one of their most popular white papers. If the consultants at the conference send prospects to this exclusive offer, they can create a digital breadcrumb trail that ties all of those prospects back to that singular conference. Without these efforts in place, the company could be wasting thousands of dollars on conferences and tradeshows that don't actually generate worthwhile leads.

Moving Forward

Now that you know how a sales funnel works, you can use this model as a guide. Take your list of marketing vehicles that you developed earlier in this book and map it to a role. It's okay if one piece, like email for example, pops up in a few different places as long as you have different initiatives within that same vehicle (one email campaign for new prospects and another email campaign for retaining customers). Once you assign those pieces, ask yourself the following questions:

- Are any stages of your sales funnel improperly equipped?
- Are any stages of your sales funnel outright failing to perform?
- What facets of your sales funnel are performing exceptionally well?
- How are you measuring each of your tactics? What data do you have and what data can you get?
- What do your competitors' sales funnels look like?

You now have a detailed plan and the context for evaluating the metrics that each of your vehicles pulls-in. Yes, your website gets a lot of traffic, but how much of that traffic is generating leads? If very little of it is converting, you can start to hone-in on an opportunity for improvement. The problem could be at either end of the connection: you might be driving a lot of traffic, but maybe it's not the right traffic. Or maybe the traffic is good but your lead magnet is not enticing enough for this particular audience. This is where the sales funnel exercise really shines. You know what you are trying to accomplish at each stage, and you can give yourself and your team a clear process for measuring your efforts.

And when you have an intimate understanding of your new business engine, you can make a more educated decision about the smartest place to innovate.

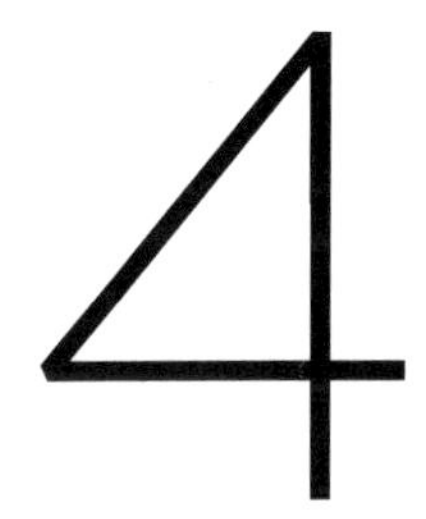

BUILDING A MARKETING PROBE

The challenge of finding a marketing niche is that the path is less traveled, or sometimes not traveled at all, which means you don't necessarily know how smoothly the trip will go. In business and in marketing, there will always be some degree of stepping into the unknown, but that feeling will be markedly stronger if you try to tap into a side door node.

That's normal, so we build exploration and testing into our process. The idea is to find a way to send out a less expensive probe before you sink a large part of your budget into a new, completely untested initiative. To be fair, this is not itself a revolutionary idea. These are industry-proven best practices that top marketing agencies and big brands routinely use to make more educated decisions. Small business owners unfortunately overlook them, sometimes because their value is not clear and sometimes because they think they can't afford to do the leg work.

If you are about to spend what you consider a significant amount of money–that exact number will be different for the family owned restaurant versus the national chain, and that's okay–you should allocate budget to testing the idea on a small scale first. It's smarter to fail at a smaller experiment. You walk away with a small bruise and more insight into your audience. If you fail at the big experiment, it can be much more painful.

In this section, we'll explore some techniques for testing your new marketing innovation before you do a full rollout. Remember that you've already done a significant amount of research, so you should already have some sense of what innovation could work based on what you've learned from your staff and from your audience. These methods will help you test that hypothesis.

That word, hypothesis, is key here. To borrow some terminology from The Lean Startup by Eric Ries, we want to develop some form of minimum viable product (MVP) to help us determine whether we should stick with our idea or go back to the drawing board to come up with something new. In the start-up world, an MVP is like a prototype but it is designed to test one part of your hypothesis, allowing you to get your product in front of a target audience as quickly as possible so that you can learn, iterate, and potentially pivot to a new idea if the response is negative. In the book, which is well-worth a read, Ries describes how Groupon tested the Groupon concept with a WordPress blog and manually emailing coupons for a pizzeria in the same building as the startup.

That's a far-cry from the mega-behemoth that Groupon became, but that low-cost test helped to prove the viability of the concept.

We want to approach marketing innovation with a similar philosophy so that we can get the most out of our marketing budget. As Ries puts it, start-ups function under "extreme uncertainty," and that's true for anyone that is trying to innovate. That's the nature of doing something new. Since we know that we're stepping out into uncharted darkness, it would seem wise that we find a way to map our next step before we bet any sizeable piece of a business on that step being safe or not.

Building A Marketing MVP

An MVP can be a difficult concept to get your hands around when you have a passion for perfection. When you like to build things that are complete and polished, putting a low-tech prototype (and Ries may take some issue with my use of prototype here, but we are working in the silo of marketing here rather than in product development so I am going to take some liberties for the sake of clarity) placeholder in front of a test audience can just feel wrong. At the same time, building a MVP takes a different kind of creativity. You have to distill your idea down to its key elements–the crucial factors that make your concept tick–to ensure that you are testing the core idea rather than the execution.

In the tech world, the MVP development tends to be more clear. A talented designer can prototype an app in a few hours, creating what almost feels like a real app but is really nothing more than a glorified Power Point. Entire software as a service platforms have been built on the back of sales that were made well before the software was even built. They armed the sales guy with a few "screenshots" of what the software will look like, and if customers put money down, well, the developers knew it was actually worth their time to make the software.

Prototyping a marketing initiative is a trickier endeavor.

How do you test a billboard without actually putting up a billboard? How do you test adding a physical storefront for your ecommerce business without actually committing to a lease? How do you test a television commercial without actually spending all of the money on production let alone on broadcast time?

There is no one-size-fits-all answer, especially as you move farther and farther into uncharted territory. And because you are stepping into uncharted territory, you might need to keep your mind open to guerilla tactics that might seem outside the scope of traditional marketing. Like I said before, testing is a creative process, so the more open and out-of-the-box your mind, the more you'll get out of this approach.

Here are some tactics that will, at the least, put you on the right path, and don't worry. We will work through examples to help put these abstract ideas into more concrete terms.

1. Find evidence to convince yourself that it will work.

The world has no shortage of devil's advocates, as Seth Godin was once said. Throughout the entire of this book, you should look for reasons why your idea will work rather than finding reasons it won't. When you're stepping into the unknown, it's all too easy to poke holes in an idea, and when you're cobbling together the most simplistic MVP of that idea possible, you will be even more tempted to put the idea down. Do the opposite. Look at your research and lay out the evidence you have for why you are on the right track.

Examples:

- Look at your audience research to remind yourself what made you think they would react positively to this idea in the first place.
- Go back over your market research to revisit the opportunity that you identified before you were faced with the challenge of developing a MVP.

- Review your competitor research to reaffirm the necessity of doing something different.

2. Identify what you're really testing.

Before you start building something to test, you need to have a clear idea of what you are trying to learn from the test. This typically means distilling your marketing idea down to one core element, the most important piece that will make or break your idea. Getting distracted by the fringe pieces that will be a part of the full launch and execution can pull your attention away from what matters most–you won't see the forest for the trees, so to speak. Ultimately, you should be able to identify where the assumptions or "leaps of faith" (as Ries puts it) are in your plan so that you can thoroughly test them.

Examples:

- A billboard is ultimately trying to capture attention in a high-traffic area, typically through a singular bold image and a simplistic piece of copy. You might be able to simulate this test with flyers or posters in a place with high foot traffic.
- If you are planning a partnership with a non-profit, you can test your audience's engagement with the cause through emails, blog posts, and social media posts where you talk about the cause but don't go as far as to commit to a formal relationship. The partnership itself is valuable, but really you're banking on your audience caring about the cause that the non-profit works to forward.
- The goal of a newspaper ad is to interrupt a reader's rhythm of moving from article to article in a positive way, usually through something eye-catching. Before you buy a full run of print ads, you might try experimenting with ad-inserts (done so manually) in a place where people might share newspapers or magazines and see what happens.
- If you're looking to test the concept behind a commercial, you might try doing a small production where you air the test on YouTube, or you might try using print ads with similar imagery and messaging.

3. Test the concept in pieces.

At the very least, break your idea down into manageable parts. We already talked about testing the core idea, and that is still critical, but testing variables within your idea can help you to refine every aspect of your idea before you do a full rollout. If the test of the core idea flopped, however, you should nail that aspect of your initiative down first. Toying with word choice on your newspaper ad won't help you if the image that occupies 95% of the space had no impact on reader attention. Whenever possible, try to leverage the speed and affordability of digital channels for your testing. This will help to keep your costs down and to accelerate your learning.

Examples:

- Use flyers, posters, and social media ads to test how your audience reacts to images.
- Use email titles, blog titles, social media posts, and pay-per-click ads to see how your audience reacts to variation in copy.
- Try variations of your ideas to see if one approach outperforms another. In the next section, we will talk about comparison testing (or A/B testing as we call it in the industry) in more depth, but variation should already be on your mind. If a particular image tests well with your audience, try to find what about tests well. Is it that people in the image? Is it the setting? Is it their expressions? If you look through stock photography, you can see how one scene can be shot in sometimes hundreds of different ways. You might be surprised how adding or removing a person in your ad affects performance.
- Test combinations of pieces that tested well already to see if you can find an exponential return. What happens if you pair that Google AdWords copy with one of your compelling images?

4. Get in front of real customers.

In the preliminary research phases, I encouraged you to talk directly to as many of your customers as you could because what your customers see and what you think your customers see are often very different. For your tests to carry any weight, you need to conduct them with your target audience. Start by engaging existing customers, preferably a nice cross-section of your base in terms of demographics and brand loyalty. Next, get in front of potential customers to see how they react to your ideas. The key here is to realize that what you, your supervisor, or your boss's wife likes is largely irrelevant when you know–through actual data–what your target audience likes. Unfortunately, creative development all-too often stays inside the vacuum of a conference room.

Examples:

- Digital marketing channels–Facebook ads, Google AdWords, email marketing, social media, YouTube ads, Reddit ads–are fast and cost-effective ways to get your marketing MVP in front of your target audience.
- Focus groups (which we will also cover in more depth in the next section) can get you candid feedback while allowing you to ask more questions about why something did or did not work the way you anticipated.
- Real world observation is a low-tech way to see how an audience might react to your idea, and if you're comfortable with going guerilla, you can do things like hang posters in public places or test your book cover by wrapping your own dust jackets around actual books at a bookstore (and seeing which covers people pick up).

5. Collect as much data as possible.

The MVP process as Ries describes it is meant to be scientific, and I argue that that approach should be the same in product development and in marketing. We want to move from gut intuition to educated decision-making as smoothly as possible, so that means collecting objective data and using that data to inform our next steps. As you test your marketing ideas with real-world customers, you should plan to collect as much intelligence as possible, so that when all of your tests are done you can make statements like "X percent of customers clicked through our ad test and became leads" or "X percent of customers found our flyer test engaging enough that they visited the website." If your team is arguing what they believe about your market rather than what the data says, your tests have missed the mark.

Examples:

- If you are testing print advertising ideas, use a unique URL coupled with a landing page to see if your test drives any traffic beyond the passing impressions you might observe in person. Alternatively, you could also try coupons or offers to track traffic to your brick & mortar store. Note: physical media can generate data, but it's often fuzzier than digital.

- For your digital efforts, use landing pages and lead generation forms to evaluate the quality of the traffic you received. If your traffic is not at the least converting to leads or adding items to their cart (some internet marketers set up a functional e-commerce presence with zero inventory just to see if people will actually go through the purchasing process), you might need to go back to the drawing board.
- If you are testing other aspects of your sales funnel, like customer service or retention, A/B testing right out of the gate might give you most insights into how well your test idea stacks up against what you do already.

6. Your ad guy might not be happy.

The marketing world is still a bit like the wild west. Anyone can open up a marketing agency and start offering services, and with remote work and freelance work more readily available because of the internet, an agency can very easily misrepresent the depth of their in-house talent pool. I know of agencies that talk about being in business for decades and having offices around the world but actually only have one fulltime employee (the owner) and divvy up the work they get to poorly paid recent college graduates or to off-shore resources. At the same time, advertising sales have become even more cut throat with the expansion of digital media, making ad executives for billboard companies and radio stations even hungrier to close sales and keep business.

While I am a big fan of agencies using freelancers and still believe that ad salespeople bring value to conversations about placement and budget and return, these institutions can struggle to keep up with your efforts at building and testing innovative marketing initiatives. The right kind of marketing agency–the one with a dedicated staff of open-minded veterans–is more likely to welcome your interest in building something unique. That's why they got into the business in the first place, and they have a wealth of experience and insights that can help you along the way. The agency that's pretending to be bigger than it is might struggle to adapt their inexperienced workforce to your new approach.

And the ad salespeople, well, they unfortunately are typically skittish when clients initiate conversations about measuring ROI or testing new ideas. The less accountability accompanying big ad spends, the more they can hide behind the number of "impressions" that your ad got rather than actually discuss whether something worked or not. If you tell someone trying to sell you billboard space that you want to hang some flyers on the subway first to see if the images resonate, they won't even know what to say.

At the end of it all, the right partners will welcome a more open and empirical approach to marketing innovation. If your consultant our agency offers you excuses rather than solutions for tracking data or testing ideas, you might consider looking for new people to work with.

Thought Experiment: MVP for a Big-Budget Idea

Earlier in the book we talked about how Apple Stores were a brilliant example of going through a side door node to reach customers in a way that Apple competitors are not. Opening Apple Stores around the world is an incredibly ambitious and costly idea to pursue. While we can see now that it was a good bet to make, anyone in the company that was present prior to this rollout would have every right to be skeptical. Other electronics companies weren't taking this path to get customers. The tasks of finding space, training staff, stocking product, and designing procedures are all large efforts in their own respects.

As an exercise, let's imagine how Apple might have used the process we described here to field test their concept before allocating a huge swath of marketing budget to the idea.

1. **Evidence that it will work:** boutique storefronts for other high-end products perform exceptionally well in part because of the carefully crafted customer experience they can provide. Though this approach was not yet present in electronics, the model hijacking template could tell us that the idea is at least worth exploring.

2. **What we're really testing:** At its core, the Apple Store concept assumes that a direct experience with Apple products coupled with the one-on-one insights from a trained Apple representative (now called "Geniuses") will deliver a better experience for customers and drive more sales. That's the heart of the idea. Yes, all of the other frills matter–like the store location, the store design, the checkout process, and product packaging–but if we distill it to down to its most essential parts, it's about getting the product into customers' hands and having a friendly knowledgeable person there to answer their questions.

3. **Testing piece by piece:** The initial MVP from Apple could be as simple as placing an Apple sales rep in the stores of a few high-traffic retailers. If the Genius is able to deliver a better Apple experience when he or she is surrounded by competitor offerings, that says a lot about the power of the experience. From there, Apple could graduate to a kiosk or "pop-up" store (perhaps renting out an unoccupied retail space temporarily) to see how a more exclusive and crafted experience performed in a mall setting. And if those tests went well, Apple could finally move into a full-on pilot store, with a full store, and a full staff to see how the idea played out over a longer period.

4. **Finding real customers:** All of the tests I just described involve real customers at every turn.

5. **Collecting data:** For these tests to generate actionable insights, Apple would need data to move from assumption to confirmation. At each stage of the hypothetical MPV described before, Apple could track foot traffic, the length of conversations, observations of customer behavior and reactions, conversion rate, and maybe even follow-up with a survey to the customers that bought. Apple could then compare this data against the numbers they already have from their retail partners and decide which approach was more effective.

This is the Cinderella version of the story, though, where all of the assumptions Apple made in this hypothetical narrative came true. If Apple had found that placing a sales rep in a store to talk directly with potential customers actually lowered their conversion rate, the marketing team would need to have a serious discussion about their ambitious plan of eventually opening Apple Stores worldwide because their core hypothesis that a direct experience with an Apple Genius would increase sales was proven to be false.

That doesn't mean that the whole idea would need to be trashed. Perhaps the approach of the salesperson could be adjusted. Perhaps the demo or display was lackluster. Perhaps it was a bad sample from a bad location. So you could run tests for those things too. If the numbers don't get better, well, it might be time to go back to the drawing board and use your new knowledge to formulate your next idea.

And look on the bright side, at least you didn't sign a 12-month lease and build out multiple stores to find out the idea wouldn't work. Hypothetically speaking of course.

5

TESTING METHODOLOGIES

I would love to give you the answer you're looking for in your business, a paint-by-numbers approach to crafting the perfect marketing plan. It doesn't exist. I've looked. So while you're on your way to discovering and perfecting the solution that is unique to your brand and unique to your market, you may need to employ a range of testing methodologies to vet and refine your plan. Some methodologies are best-suited for certain types of ideas and may become wholly impractical when applied to other ideas.

Thinking creatively about your marketing is a skill that takes practice. Seasoned marketers develop an intuition for how best to evaluate and test their ideas, and you'll get there to. For now, here are some suggestions that will make our work easier in the long run:

- Make the goals of your tests clear to your team members so that they can contribute constructively to the execution.
- Take the time to plan out your test before actually building anything. Yes, an MVP should be quick, but that's relative to the full-scale launch. Your MVP should still be well-designed so that it tests the right hypothesis.
- Know what sort of data you want to gather and make sure that your MVP will generate that data.
- Just because you use a test once doesn't mean you can't use it again.
- Don't be afraid to mix and match your testing methodologies to get different

kinds of insights.

- Check that your systems and analytics are functioning properly. For example, I've seen ecommerce stores pour thousands of dollars into testing only to discover that Google Analytics was not installed properly on key pages of the site.

Now let's explore some of the testing methodologies at your disposal so that you can get the most from your MVP and for testing the efficacy of your idea as you get closer and closer to the final version.

The One-Off

Try something new in a low-stakes setting and compare it your existing data.

This is where most MVPs are born and where most MVPs die. We've discussed the best practices of MVPs already, and I won't rehash them already. Instead, we should talk about how one-offs are different from other testing methodologies. The biggest difference: the quality of your data.

Think of the one-off as a pilot program. When you do a one-off test, your only frame of reference will be the data you've collected historically from previous but likely completely unrelated marketing activities. You might be able say with some reasonable certainty if your new idea performed better than previous ideas, but that's about as far as you can draw your conclusions. You won't have the context to definitively say why the idea worked.

To take the one-off apart and determine what variables really make it work, you will need to use other testing methodologies. Depending on the idea you're exploring, either A/B testing or focus grouping (or perhaps both) may be best. For the one off stage itself, here are somethings to keep in mind:

- One-offs are usually either MPVs or the first big official push for a new marketing idea, where you have a pretty good sense for how well the new initiative will work but still aren't ready to go all-in. If the one-off MVP flops, you can go into A/B testing to maybe figure out why, but you might be better off just going back to the drawing board.
- For early tests, run your one-off tests in a closed, semi-controlled setting rather than exposing your entire audience (or prospective audience) to what could

turn out to be a bad idea. Digital marketing tools make this easy, but physical marketing can take more creativity.

- The overall goal of a one-off is to find a justification to continue down the path of exploring an idea. If a one-off goes well, you probably shouldn't skip ahead to a massive launch. Instead, you should ramp up with progressively larger tests.
- If you can't figure out a way to push a one-off out into the market in a controlled way, you might consider running the one-off with a focus group or with one of the guerilla testing approaches I cover later.

A/B Testing

Run two very similar tests simultaneously; Compare the results.

Digital marketing channels are so powerful that they feel like magic. Unlike print media, you can test a digital ad for a really small amount of money. The entry price for a billboard in some major markets can be upward of $23,000 for a 4-week run. That's a lot of money to spend on an ad that you're not sure will work.

With Facebook ads or Google AdWords, you can do a targeted test of copy and images for a few hundred dollars. Better yet, you can compare the performance of one ad against another by running them simultaneously and shutdown one ad or both at your discretion.

This is a classic digital marketing technique that you can use for your ads, your websites, your emails, and your content. The process is relatively straightforward: pick a single variable that you want to test–like a headline or a title or a button placement–and see which version performs better. The drawback to A/B testing is that it works best for incremental change rather than large abrupt changes. At the same time, the drawback is a strength:

When you have the sense that you are on a good path, A/B testing can be a great way to refine and mold your idea. Once you've collected enough data to determine that one is more effective than the other, you can move forward with implementing the better version or with your next variable test.

A great deal has been written about A/B testing in books and in blogs online, so you can spend a great deal of time learning strategies and techniques for getting the most of this process.

For our purposes, here are some tips and best practices to get you started:

- Traditional A/B testing mandates that you create two versions where only one variable is different. If you change more than one variable, you will no longer be able to attribute improvements in performance to a single factor. You can A/B test any variable related to your initiative, whether it's the design, placement, targeting, or follow-up.
- When you're choosing variables to test, start with the biggest variables first. For example, the headline on an ad or the image are more important to dial-in than smaller script that might accompany the ad. For an email, testing the email title before you test the body will give you more bang for your buck as well since people decide whether or not to open the email based on the title. Ask yourself what people will see first or what is most important and start there.
- Run your tests against the same audience. If you are testing email design, for example, split your email list randomly and send half one version of the email and half the other version of the email. The only exception to this rule is if you are testing audience targeting with a platform like Facebook, but even then the audience should be mostly the same.
- You need users to glean a meaningful insight. If your test audience is too small, you might misinterpret an anomaly as a trend. Digital marketing gurus each have their own benchmarks for how much traffic you need to really say that one thing is definitively better than another thing. The challenge for small businesses is that their audience won't be anywhere near as large as that of a brand like Amazon, so how much is really enough? You should probably start with at least 1000. You can work with less, but you should be more and more careful about how much you trust a conclusion the smaller your audience gets.
- Stay mindful of the metrics you're tracking. Keep your entire sales funnel in mind. Just because version A drove more clicks than version B does not mean that version A will generate more profit. Myself and the marketers I've worked with have seen many cases where one vehicle will dramatically outperform another vehicle at one of these upfront metrics but actually produces less business in the long run. These metrics are still valuable, but don't take the easy way out and stop there. You might end up launching something that creates a ton of conversation but actually does very little to grow the business.

- Technically, you can A/B test physical media and campaigns as well, but getting a true 50/50 split in your audience is more difficult and the data can become less empirical. It still may be worth pursuing, however.

Focus Groups

Gather feedback from a captive segment of your target audience.

Many marketers leapfrog the focus group process because of the logistics. To conduct an effective focus group you need to get people from your target audience into one room at the same time, which can mean renting conference space at a more centralized location (for your audience) and bribing them with some sort of offer (a gift card, lunch, maybe both). Then you need a moderator who is skilled at steering conversation and collecting meaningful feedback.

That amount of work discourages a lot of people from using focus groups, and that's a mistake.

In terms of collecting feedback and data, you can get pretty far with A/B testing and follow up surveys, but the limitations of these tools is that you can't follow up with more in depth questions about why someone reacted the way they did.

Having the chance to ask direct questions to your target audience can uncover opportunities you might have missed otherwise. While this feedback is not statistically significant like A/B test results (which is quantitative whereas focus groups are qualitative), it can reveal a new path for you to test.

Don't let the work involved deter you. Like we've discussed before: a little work now can save you a lot of budget later.

If you opt to run a focus group, keep these best practices in mind:

- Focus groups should ideally be between 5 to 10 people so that each participant is more likely to contribute and ideally react to the feedback of others. The larger your focus group gets, the more likely you are to start a collective conversation.
- The quality of your moderator is the linchpin of the focus group. A moderator should make participants feel comfortable and safe while also knowing how and when to steer conversation. A focus group moderator has the delicate task of talking just enough to keep the discussion moving and not talking so much

that he or she biases the responses from focus group participants.

- Your focus group should be a representative sample of your target audience unless of course you are testing a specific segment of your customer base. Diversity in your focus group can mean multiple viewpoints, which hopefully means more conversation about the idea you're testing. If a focus group turns into an echo chamber of everyone agreeing, you either hit a homerun, failed definitively, or created an echo chamber.
- Have a script prepared ahead of time that describes the goal of the focus group and includes a collection of questions that you'd like to ask. Try to be concise. The temptation to ask about everything will be strong, but your discussion should revolve around what you're aiming to test, whether you're testing an MVP or a near-complete project.
- Don't be afraid to deviate from the script to explore something unexpected. This is the beauty of focus groups, but an inexperienced moderator will run past the opportunity to go deeper to ask the next question on the list.
- You may need to run multiple focus groups over the course of development or to get a good sense of how your audience actually feels about something. If you're doing multiple iterations, you should be able to chart some progress from group to group.

Guerilla Field Tests

Force your idea into the real world to see how people react.

We touched on a few varieties of guerilla field tests in our exploration of developing a MVP, but I want to explore some options in greater detail here because these can be great ways to get your ideas in front of an uninformed audience so that you can get unbiased reactions. I'm a big fan of these approaches because they are typically low-tech and a lot of fun to execute. At the same time, the raw reaction of a totally unprepared test subject can be enlightening.

Fair warning, these tests are almost entirely qualitative, but that doesn't make them less useful. When someone enters a focus group, they are prepared and might even filter some of their feedback. An A/B test gives you some great data, but since much of it happens digitally you won't see how your users reacts.

You'll have to imagine what went into each action, which takes us back to the weird and dangerous world of assuming things.

If you make an observation during a guerilla test, use that as a starting point for more quantitative research. Oh, and I don't advocate doing anything illegal for your guerilla test, and I definitely don't advocate getting caught. Some ideas for how you can use guerilla marketing tests:

- Public transportation terminals are a great place to hang "unofficial" flyers or posters and see how people react. Make sure you have some sort of unique URL or coupon code tied to them to see if they actually drive an action beyond catching someone's eye.
- If you're testing packaging of some sort, actually put your product on a shelf in a large store. To actually get anything out of this, you'll need a high-traffic location at a busy time, and you might need to switch off with an observer if there is not a natural place to hangout nearby.
- Set up a booth at a craft show or flea market. You'll have to fork over a little bit of money here, but if you're in a B2C space you can crash test your sales pitch as well as your promotional materials. Bonus points if you set up two booths at either end and use completely different promotional materials and company names to see what happens.
- Host an event without telling the venue. If you're not sure whether or not your audience will come out for an event, piggy back on an event your audience would care about and advertise an after party at a club of your choice without telling them what you're planning. Ask guests to check in with a certain person (share a picture) for a reward.

Hire Testers

Pay customers to go through your sales process and give you feedback.

This is the secret shopper model, but you can apply the same approach to testing your new marketing. Hiring testers is different from focus groups in that you can do it almost 100% hands off. You set up the experience, send them or direct them to what they need to test, and then collect their feedback afterward via a survey or follow-up interview (if you want more depth).

If your marketing idea is buried deep in your sales funnel, this can be the most efficient way to get a significant number of users through each stage without having to wait a long time or spend a bunch of money on advertising (which could be frustrating if that piece ends up not working).

The drawback to this approach as that your users are preselected in some way, potentially biasing the feedback you get. This is a fair concern, but I would actually encourage you to use that to your advantage. If you are sending a troupe of testers through your marketing campaign to get their feedback, these are people that either care enough about your business or your industry that they want to be involved with the process of shaping it–likely a crowd of early adopters or passionate advocates–or they are experienced testers that have the experience and language necessary to identify and describe problems you might not have considered.

The volume of feedback that you stand to gain from this testing approach should be useful in your decision-making to either move forward with your idea or to make an adjustment. To get the best possible feedback, keep the following in mind:

- Since the power of this approach is that you don't have to hand-hold each individual tester, you will likely rely on some sort of automated feedback gathering system (probably a digital survey tool of some sort). Before you deploy your test, do a few dry-runs internally to make sure that everything (from the first email to the final survey collection) is working properly.
- Brush up on survey best practices to get the most out of your feedback. Avoid open ended or confusing questions. Keep the survey brief (no more than 20 questions; shorter if you can pull it off). Keep the demographic questions fair and put them at the end.
- When you do send your test out, keep the initial explanation prompt brief and objective. Simply explain what you're doing and why, and be careful not to give too much flavor. You might end up biasing the responses if you aren't careful
- If you aren't sure where to find testers, start with a collection of your best customers. This shows that you value their feedback, that you care about maintaining the integrity of the brand that they already love, and that you recognize their role in your continued success. At the same time, it's quite likely that your customers understand your brand better than you do.
- Hire testers online. Multiple services offer to give you the kinds of testers you

are looking for a fee that tends to be reasonable (especially if your test is vetting the concept for a big budget project down the road). Before you send a check out, however, look up reviews for the company you are talking to and ask them how they get their testers. An army of bots or off-shore workers going through your test won't be helpful.

- Some test settings lend themselves well to recording, either via webcam or in person. This approach starts to take you closer to being a focus group, but you can cycle people through relatively quickly and follow-up with survey to gather feedback quickly. If you have the budget, investing in some eye-tracking tools could give you a stronger sense for how and what people are reacting to in an ad or on a website.
- The most pointless survey question is "Would you buy this?" Answering yes to that question is much different from actually pulling your wallet out and buying. If you need to use this question in your testing–and you probably will in many cases–call your survey-takers bluff. Give them the option to buy the product right then and there and see what happens.

MVP Examples and Tests

Talking in the abstract is useful to a point, but with so much of the MVP process hinging upon you applying these concepts to your unique business we need to work through some concrete examples to bring these ideas to life. By seeing how other businesses might build and test a MVP, my hope is that you will start to see how you can too.

Valve Software

In this story, we talked about how a video game development studio built the iTunes for video games: Steam. Earlier, we talked about how Valve initially launched the platform as a sort of digital rights management (DRM) system, requiring all players of Half-Life 2 to install the client before playing one of the most anticipated games in the history of video games. The initial explanation for Steam was that it was going to be a streamlined process for delivering patches and software updates.

That was in 2002. Valve did not bring in third party developers until 2005. In those three years, Steam was used exclusively for Valve titles. Think about that: Valve spent three years nursing a platform that had the potential to transform video game sales as we knew it. Valve didn't immediately fill their digital store shelves with other products. They didn't aggressively pursue new partnerships.

They sold their own games–powerhouses in the industry but a very small sliver of the available titles–and their own games only. This turned out to be a smart move because their growing pains were significant. Users immediately complained about the restrictions of DRM. The steam client was buggy.

And when Valve made the push to only sell their games through Steam, well, that was the coming of the apocalypse for some gamers. The word of mouth reputation for Steam was so bad at one point that fans started sharing an animation where the Steam logo repeatedly inserted itself into an orifice of one poor gentleman.

It would seem, from the outside, that Valve followed the MVP model. Their digital storefront didn't start with thousands of games from publishers and developers around the world. It started with a few. At the same time, Valve made a distinct choice to persevere despite that sometimes significant volume of negative feedback they got for what Steam did and how it worked. I suspect they made that decision based on the data they were collecting from the platform.

Sure, some users were vocal about their distaste for Steam, but gamers were using it to buy and play games. Those are the key metrics for Valve, and to me, that's what Valve was ultimately testing. As long as those metrics were going up, the rest of the challenges–like user feedback–could be addressed constructively.

I feel pretty confident that this is part of Valve's process because recently Valve pushed another MVP into the world. They rolled out a new way to distribute fan-made content (called "mods" in the community). Instead of making the change platform-wide, Valve implemented it for one game, **Skyrim**.

The experiment flopped, costing the company at least millions in just four days–the loss of revenue was a mix of man hours wasted dealing with a flood of emails and messages as well as some ad hoc protests against Valve and its platform Steam. In that time, Gabe Newell, Valve CEO said that they only generated $10,000 a profit. So Valve killed the idea, and in so doing, demonstrated how it decides whether or not to persevere: despite complaints, what are our sales numbers?

To launch Steam, Valve built a mini version of what the platform became. They rolled out it their audience of fans, people who loved and would buy their games no matter what (one-off). When they saw traction, they continued expanding the platform and gathering feedback (A/B tests and tester feedback). Then they turned they added on to their model hijacking template by expanding the platform to include partnerships with third party developers after they had spent three years iterating on improvements.

That's not too shabby.

Sarris Candies

Hidden in my earlier retelling of the Sarris Candies story was a one-off MVP. Like Valve's Steam platform, Sarris did not begin their new sales strategy with a company-wide rollout. They didn't send letters or salespeople to nonprofit directors or to local businesses. They didn't build a formal fundraising package with branded boxes and glossy brochures.

Instead, they armed a small group of kids, who were passionate about their cause of raising money for their class–with some candy bars. This one-off MVP demonstrated the viability of fundraising as a marketing tactic. The only risk to the business was potentially wasting product, and even that could be mitigated by giving the students limited inventor to start and replenishing their stock as they sold it.

I love this story because it's so beautifully low tech. This entire program could be tested with a few envelopes, some product that's already been made, and a notebook. Today, it would be tempting to test this idea by designing everything that could go into it. The Sarris fundraising program as it exists now features special boxes for carrying candy bars as well as beautiful designed candy catalogs and order sheets all backed by a streamlined system for tracking purchases and distributing funds back to fundraisers.

All of those pieces are important, but they are not the cornerstone of what makes the model effective. Whether or not they realized it at the time, the Sarris family was really testing whether cause-related marketing would sell more candy. That's it. Everything else that comes later hinges upon that key idea. When you know for sure that a young smiling face talking about her class trip or how her softball team needs new equipment not only moves product but makes customers more loyal to your brand, you can figure everything else out later.

When that idea was proven, Sarris could move on to testing and iterating on everything else. Now that they have a website and a broad customer base, I wouldn't be surprised if they have A/B tested how they talk about and how they format their fundraising programs and materials. They have probably had focus groups with nonprofit and community leaders about how they could better serve them. And they have likely gathered mountains of feedback and data from their customers and as well as their fundraising partners.

Sega

How do you convince an underdog video game company to book a hotel, fly-in staff, and spend thousands of dollars on new promotional material for a retailer-exclusive event in Florida?

You run a series of tests.

As you will recall from earlier in this book, one of Sega's biggest challenges was coping with the marketing momentum of the industry-leading Nintendo. Nintendo controlled most of the retailers, they had the biggest presence at key industry expos, and they were so well-established that they could typically one-up Sega in every traditional channel by simple virtue of being bigger and having been around longer.

Instead of making their next big announcement at the expo where Nintendo had dominated in the past, Sega made the bold (and expensive) decision to host their own conference a few months earlier. This piece of marketing brilliance was a product of a series of small tests and victories and emboldened by a clear need to find a different way of competing with the Nintendo behemoth.

Prior to their invite-only Sega mini-conference in Florida, Sega had tested pieces of their idea by:

- Talking with dozens of key retail managers and distributors to under their pain points and what they want out of a partnership with a company like Sega.
- Touring the country with a Nintendo vs. Sega event that let gamers play both systems and say which ones they liked better.
- Running a range of ads, trying to dial-in Sega's brash brand personality so that it resonated with gamers.
- Following up with retailers with a never-say-die approach to sales, going as fire to rent every billboard around the Walmart headquarters to open the door.

In addition to these insights, Sega also knew where it had lost to Nintendo, and that was just as valuable as knowing what had worked. If the biggest electronics expo in the world could make or break the company, well, that was too big of a bet to make. So they took all of the learning from their other experiments and decided that they had enough evidence to support that this idea would work.

And it did.

Sears

The idea to print a smaller catalog was likely born from a simple observation: When someone stacks up the magazines and catalogs on their coffee table, they tend to put the largest on the bottom and then stack upward according to size, going from the largest to the smallest. The observation is one thing, but investing in an entire print run for the pivotal driver of your business is another.

If Sears wanted to develop an MVP for this idea, they could take a few different approaches.

First, they could take a guerilla testing approach and plant a few of their catalogs in places where there were a lot of magazines: like a doctor's office. With or without the permission of the doctor, a representative from Sears could observe for a few hours. What happens when someone tidies up the office? And if the catalog ends up stacked at the top, does that mean people are more likely to reach for it first?

If that test went well, Sears could roll out a second test. By finding two similar markets with similar purchase habits and sales volume, Sears could send one market the smaller version and the other market the regular version. This A/B test is a bit more expensive than sitting in a doctor's office, but the risk is much lower than if Sears had switched over the entire country in one swipe. With this test, Sears could see if the smaller catalog got more attention at the top of the pile and if that attention generated more sales.

If the answer is yes, this smaller catalog does increase sales, then Sears could probably have the insight they need to do a full launch. If there were still reservations, Sears could follow up their A/B test with surveys to see what customers thought of the new catalog in the off chance that there was some hidden problem, but the first two tests allow Sears to demonstrate to themselves that the smaller catalog will end up at the top of the pile and that this mechanic actually increases sales.

From there, the opportunity is likely in streamlining the contents, which could lead to more tests and experiments with photos, copy, pricing, shipping options, and so forth, but the two MVPs got the company this far (in our hypothetical analysis), and that turned into a big win.

The PT Services Group

When PT mailed out 200 paperbacks (rather than an e-book) to augment their already powerful new business services, they know from the start that it was a pilot program. They didn't know how it would work when it came to cold calls, but they had reason to believe it would help.

Their partner, Charlie Epstein of 401k Coach, had been field testing a book as a sales tool for years. He had seen it work in his own business and in the businesses of the advisors he helped, so it was reasonable to assume that mailing out paperbacks to prospects prior to a call would improve conversion rates. But that word, assumption, should be the trigger for a MVP, and that's exactly what PT did.

Printing and mailing 200 books is not exactly cheap, but it's far cheaper than printing and mailing enough books for every single client that PT serves, and it's safer than putting the effectiveness of all of their work at risk for the sake of implementing a new idea. The pilot worked in a big way, but there are still opportunities to continue testing. The most immediate opportunity would be to interview the prospects that agreed to an appointment. Did they read the book? What resonated with them? Was the content of the book what made them take the appointment or was it simply that the advisor seemed more reputable because he had his own book? Was this approach a powerful play on reciprocity?

Those 200 books were a one-off. PT knows it worked, but pinning down exactly why requires a bit more learning. When PT has the data to conclusively say what about the book made it a more effective marketing tool, they can build on that and amplify the return they see. This could be as simple as using a different book cover or as involved as the advisor running more workshops and events in the area, but it's difficult to say without more learning.

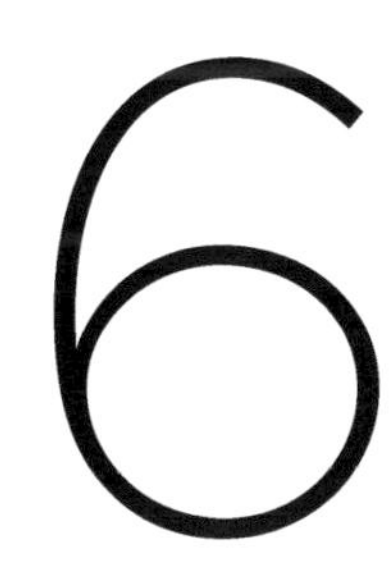

3... 2... 1...

Launch. That's a scary word. You've done all of this research, planning, and testing, and now you are placing your bet. You are sending the thing you built out into the world, and it's different. It's not like the other kids in the class. She's a bit weird. She makes strange comparisons and dresses differently. You love her because she's your kid, and you did your best to raise her right, but she's so distinctly separate from the typical blueprint that you just don't know how she will turn out.

When you do something different, you don't have an industry standard to measure it against because you are setting the new standard. You're the first one into the darkness, and the only map you have is the one you are sketching as you go.

That might be a bit dramatic, but I am sensitive to the fact that your business could mean everything to you. It's how you feed your family, and it's how you plan to put your kids through college. With these sorts of stakes, I think taking a step back to appreciate the gravity of what we are about to do is not only fair, it's healthy. You are operating a powerful tool, so you treat it with the respect that comes from understanding that tool can do tremendous good and at the same time do tremendous damage.

This is the point where I struggle with a large portion of the agency world. I have sat in meetings where the lead on the account pushed the client to invest even more money into the monthly retainer because that extra $4,000 was what would turn the tide and bring in more revenue (according to the account lead). Never mind that the client, a small family business, had already expressed that times were getting tougher and the already sizeable budget was straining other aspects of their business. Never mind that if this advice was bad that it could actually send the business into a death spiral.

The most important thing–in the mind of the account lead–is growing the account. That's it.

As you become your own ad hoc marketing director with the help of this book or arm yourself with the vocabulary and insights you need to be a more active participant in the plans that your agency or outside consultant are building for your business, there are a few realities that you should always keep in mind as you near the lunch of your next big marketing idea. These aren't meant to scare you or discourage you. Instead, this is the honest conversation that every agency should have with its clients but doesn't because it's uncomfortable and might not lead to a bigger retainer.

1. **This might not work.** The second you commit to innovation you become an explorer. By stepping into the unknown, you can't say for sure how well your plan will work, adding even more uncertainty to an industry where uncertainty is already the norm. Innovation is driven by experimentation, and experiments often fail. If you want the treasure that no one has, you have to risk a boulder coming down the hallway after you.

2. **Don't bet the house.** I first heard this piece of advice from a Seth Godin podcast called Start-Up School, and it's stuck with me. He was talking about business rather than marketing, but I think the wisdom applies to marketing as well. If you ever get to the point where you are treating your next marketing initiative like the last hand of a bad night of poker–this will be the hand that wins me back all the money I lose–take a step back immediately. You're not thinking clearly and are putting too much on the line.

3. **People naturally resist change.** Any time you buck the status quo, you invite criticism. Most of that criticism will be driven by a deeply rooted fear of change that will inspire turmoil whether or not the change is good. The early stages of your rollout will be awkward, and you may need to do some fine tuning here and there to really dial-in your execution, but don't let yourself get spooked. Persevere and give your idea a chance to work.

4. **Monitor data throughout.** The sales funnel analysis and MVP process should

have given you a practice identifying measurable points in your campaign and using that data to create actionable insights. You should do this throughout your campaign and be willing to learn from it on the fly. If something goes really wrong or goes really write you want to know as early as possible so you can respond appropriately.

5. **Be ready to capture momentum.** A marketing campaign is not a rocket where you do all of the calculations and preparation up front so that you can sit back and watch it soar into the sky after launch. Instead, think of your work as a sailboat. Winds will change, and if you catch a particularly good wind, you want to capitalize. How exactly you can capture momentum will vary by campaign, but at the very least you shouldn't go on vacation at this point in time, and you should be monitoring your email and social media for engagement.

It's time. You did the work. You ran the tests. You found your opportunity to be bold and stand out. Seize it.

POST-LAUNCH

Congratulations. You accomplished what 99% of marketers fail to do in their careers: you did something different. You made a conscious effort to break from the pack to connect with your target audience. Your work as a marketer, however is just beginning.

With your new idea in the world generating conversation and engagement, you have opened the door to a wealth of new learning opportunities. You are collecting a new stream of data. You are connecting with new customers. And you are gathering feedback on this bold new initiative that you introduced to the market. If this feels familiar, that's because it is. This is the start of a new innovation research process, which will turn into a new round of testing and iteration if you follow through with the process.

You should, without a doubt, follow through with the process.

Becoming an innovative brand is not about conquering one innovation. Rather, innovation needs to become a part of your brand's DNA. It has to be rooted deeply into your culture and how you and your team approaches business growth. Innovators never stop innovating. They are always thinking, testing, and creating. They never stop looking at the world around them and imagining how they could do something different within it.

As we talked about throughout this book, innovation does not always have to be world changing idea. Instead, it can be a small twist on something existing, adding just enough of a different perspective to make the old way new again. With the innovation that you just launched, you might spend the next few years evolving that idea, teasing it out in a new ways and pushing the envelope at specific, strategic points. Or, maybe after a year you explore a new avenue.

The more you make innovation who you are as a business leader, the more you train your customers to think of your brand as an innovator. They come to expect new ideas from you, and they will even begin to look forward to it. Customers are often looking for leaders to follow, and leaders rarely stand still rehashing the same, tired ideas.

So crack open your notebook again and get to work. You're an innovator now.

Get to innovating.

APPENDIX

HELPFUL RESOURCES

Books

The Challenger Sale: Taking Control of the Customer Conversation by Matthew Dixon and Bren Adamson. Portfolio. November, 2011.

Relationship selling has gone the way of the dinosaur. The challenger framework is not only more effective for sales, but it provides a unique framework for structuring your marketing messages as well.

Console Wars: Sega, Nintendo, and the Battle that Defined a Generation by Blake J. Harris. Dey Street Books. June, 2015.

Console wars is a play by play of how Sega and Nintendo battled for the worldwide video game market. On the surface, it's a book about video game culture, but really it's the most in-depth play-by-play analysis of big brand marketing that I've ever read.

The 4-Hour Workweek: Escape 9-5, Live Anywhere, and Join the New Rich by Timothy Ferriss. Harmony. December 2009.

Perhaps has a reputation for being a bit out there, and that might be deserved. Despite the hyperbole of this book title, 4-Hour Workweek is one of the best resources on quick and dirty marketing tactics available, summarizing many of today's standard internet marketing strategies into one book.

Good to Great: Why Some Companies Make the Leap...And Other's Don't by Jim Collins. HarperBusiness. October, 2001.

For me, the idea that marketing and the way a business operates at its core began with reading this book. When the identify of your business is healthy and well-defined and you have the right people working with you, an honest and engaging marketing strategy is easier to build.

Great by Choice: Uncertainty, Chaos, and Luck–Why Some Thrive Despite Them All by Jim Collins. HarperBusiness. October, 2011.

Written in the same vein as his previous work, this book from Collins continues to explore what makes great companies tick. Those insights, in my mind, influence the marketing choices we make in our businesses every day.

Guerilla Marketing: Easy and Inexpensive Strategies for Making Big Profits from Your Small Business by Jay Conrad Levinson with Jeannie and Amy Levinson. Houghton Mifflin. May 2007).

This classic marketing book, despite its age, is a great source of creative inspiration for finding new, less-expensive paths to connect with your target audience. There are additional iterations and editions are as well.

The Lean Startup: How Today's Entrepreneurs Use Continuous Innovation to Create Radically Successful Businesses by Eric Ries. Crown Business. September, 2011.

The Lean Startup changed how I thought about data and about how I build anything business related. The work that Ries has done is relevant for every business of every size and will help you to think differently about how you make business decisions.

Purple Cow: Transform Your Business by Being Remarkable by Seth Godin. Portfolio. May 2003.

Perhaps the original "be different" marketing book, Purple Cow is a rallying cry to think outside of the box and to challenge yourself and your business to do something bold and unique.

Unleashing the Ideavirus: Stop Marketing AT People! Turn Your Ideas into Epidemics by Helping Your Customers Do the Marketing Thing for You by Seth Godin. Hachette Books. October, 2001.

Can you tell I'm a Seth Godin fan? Ideavirus understood viral marketing before the internet did and thoroughly explores why customers talk about the things they love and how you can inspire them to spread the word about your work.

UnMarketing: Stop Marketing. Start Engaging by Scott Stratten and Alison Kramer. Wiley. February, 2012.

Real marketing is greater than the sum of its part. It's about engaging customers in meaningful ways, and UnMarketing sets out to help you see the dangers of getting lost in your dashboard while at the same time giving you inspiration for bringing more humanity into your outreach.

Podcasts

Seth Godin's Start-Up School: http://www.earwolf.com/show/startup-school/

This is a podcast in the loosest sense of the word. Godin ran a boot camp of sorts for entrepreneurs and recorded his lecturers. Each episode is densely packed with business insights and practical advice. I listen to this series a few times a year.

This Week in Start-Ups: http://thisweekinstartups.com/

Host Jason Calacanis has a strong personality that some users dislike, but his interviews are phenomenal. His guests hail from a range of businesses around the start-up world, and their candid discussions of their businesses, their challenges, and what they've learned from their work could give you a new insight into your own business.

The Tim Ferriss Show: http://fourhourworkweek.com/podcast/

Despite his polarizing reputation, Ferriss has a knack for connecting with exceptional people. His podcast is a treasure trove of conversations with some of the best and brightest business minds on the planet.

Nerdist Podcast: http://nerdist.com/podcasts/nerdist-podcast-channel/

The brainchild of comedian turned media mogul Chris Hardwick, the Nerdist Podcast typically interviews actors and other celebrities, but even those talks often uncover insights into the creative process that could be helpful to your business.

REFERENCES

"Bill Sarris manages growth at Sarris Candies with a dollop of old-fashioned values" by Jayne Gest. *Smart Business Online.* October 1, 2014. (http://www.sbnonline.com/article/bill-sarris-manages-growth-sarris-candies-dollop-old-fashioned-values/)

"Full Steam Ahead: The History of Valve" by Jeff Dunn. *Gamesradar+.* October 4, 2013. (http://www.gamesradar.com/history-of-valve/)

"The Sears, Roebuck and Co. Complex, North Lawndale" by Caroline Nye Stevens. *Blueprint: Chicago.* April 23, 2012. (http://www.blueprintchicago.org/2012/04/23/the-sears-roebuck-co-complex-north-lawndale/)

"Steam Sales 2015: Valve Has Generated a Total of $3.5 Billion from Paid Games" by Abdul Haddi. *GearNuke.* January 6, 2016. (http://gearnuke.com/steam-sales-2015-valve-generated-total-3-5-billion-paid-games/#)

"Valve CEO: 'Pissing off the internet costs you a million bucks in just a couple of days'" by Dave Smith. *Business Insider.* April 28, 2015. (http://www.businessinsider.com/valve-ends-paid-skyrim-mods-2015-4)

Bonus Content: Precision Social Media

This was originally written as an independent e-book and I've included it here to help you with your standard social media marketing strategy as well as to help you think about how you could potentially use your social media in more innovative ways. Enjoy.

Introduction to Precision Social Media

If you are a business owner, you are always hearing about silver bullets. If you only had an app, if you only had better search engine rankings, if you only had a Facebook page–you would be rich. Customers would be beating down your door, and orders would be spilling out of your inbox. The reality is, however, that you have limited time and limited resources. You cannot chase every new piece of marketing magic and still run a successful business.

Social media is not a silver bullet, but overlooking it could mean missing a valuable (and profitable) opportunity to connect directly with your customers. Social media at its best is a vehicle for fostering relationships with customers. You can engage in meaningful conversations that can lead to increased brand loyalty, referrals, and conversions.

Social media empowers you to turn your customers into vocal advocates for your business, products, or services. But where do you start?

You Don't Need to be Everything to Everyone

In this e-book, we aim to bring clarity to social media marketing, giving you a basic guide for choosing how and where you invest your social media resources. We summarize the major social platforms, explore their strengths and weaknesses, and talk briefly about what types of audiences you can expect find on each. In our experience, social media marketing is most effective when it is conducted with precision. We have had more success tailoring our approach to a specific audience rather than trying to talk as loudly as possible on every platform available.

Your target audience will respond to a message aimed directly at them, and your commitment to precision will maximize the return that you get on your messaging.

Here are the key elements of the precision social media philosophy:

- Use only the platforms that are relevant to your brand and that you have the resources to maintain.
- Know that an unattended or abandoned social media property can become a liability for your business.
- Understand and utilize the appropriate posting frequency for your chosen platforms.
- Leverage the unique functionality of each platform instead of taking a one-size-fits-all approach to posting.
- Social media is about conversation, so use your social presence to do more than advertise your latest products or sales.

Social media is a powerful tool, but for it to be effective for your business it must be executed in a way that makes sense for your goals and for your audience.

General Best Practices

To get the most out of your social media marketing, you should immerse yourself in the unique functionality of your chosen platforms. Knowing the nuances of using Twitter versus the nuances of using Facebook can give you more credibility and help you to better connect with your target audiences. As you think about what platforms to choose and how you'd like to use them, there are some general best practices that apply to virtually every social media marketing initiative.

- Quality always trumps quantity. Social media users are a savvy bunch, and they are sensitive to brands spamming their feeds or inbox. If your content is not genuine and interesting, don't share it.
- Post natively. You can potentially daisy-chain multiple platforms together so that one post on Facebook gets shared to Twitter which gets shared to your Google+, but this approach ultimately punishes your super fan (the one that follows you on everything). Post natively to each platform you use to take advantage of the conventions and functionality unique to each of them.
- Remember that you are representing a business. That means being careful about what you say and also posting content that matches the quality of what you are trying to sell. This could mean picking up a nicer smartphone or hiring a graphic designer to spruce up your graphics.
- Be agile. Respond quickly to user comments and feedback and stay up to date on changes coming to your favorite platforms. If you are slow to react, your followers could lose interest or respect.
- Follow a schedule. Make a plan ahead of time so that you know what you plan to post on each day of a week. This will save you having to start from scratch each day. It's not a bad idea to generate content ahead of time, but there is also value in being spontaneous.
- Be wary of buying an audience. Paying for social ads that grow your follower count or number of likes can lead to a large audience that has no actual interest in your business. Paying a service to grow your audience is even worse. Focus more on making great content and sharing that content in places where your audience congregates.
- Measure your efforts. Generate regular reports on your efforts. Look at what posts garnered the most interest and the most conversions. Use this data to inform your strategy changes over time.

These general tips will set you down a good path. Once you have picked the social platforms you plan to adopt, using the guide that follows in the next chapter, seek out experts on each to learn the best practices that are platform specific.

Platform Overviews

Facebook

Facebook has become the undisputed king of social media. Facebook has the largest number of users and has a strong international following in addition to its US user-base. Furthermore, Facebook has a history of acquiring other social media networks and has strong API support, which means that your other social and business tools probably integrate with Facebook in some way. At the same time, Facebook has adopted an aggressive approach to monetizing its business potential, making it more difficult for fan page owners to reach their fans for free.

Audience: Facebook users are numerous and hail from a range of demographics, but as more social media networks enter the market, the age of Facebook users appears to be skewing toward an over 30 crowd, though we are just at the beginning of this shift. It's worth noting this because you may need to pick a different platform if you specifically plan on targeting younger customers.

Posting Tips:

- Post once or twice a day. Posting a large volume of content with poor engagement can hurt your overall exposure.
- Use Facebook Insights to determine the ideal posting time for your audience.
- Post worthwhile, quality content that drives engagement to improve how many of your fans actually see your content.
- Always target ads. A generic "Get Likes" ad can lead to inflating your likes with fake Facebook fans, which means even less of your actual fans will see your posts.
- Do not use hashtags. They actually hurt your engagement and make your posts look silly.
- If you make videos, upload them directly to Facebook to increase your engagement on Facebook (still uploading to YouTube is a good idea).

- If you are sharing links, customize the pre-populated attachment (title, photo, and summary) to make it as attractive as possible to your fans.

Strengths:

- The potential audience is huge, encompassing a wide variety of demographics and interests.
- Used by a number of brands (mostly B2C) already, so customers are used to being marketed to via Facebook.
- Robust advertising tools give businesses the power to target and retarget narrowly defined demographic criteria.
- The Facebook beacon campaign is promising for brick and mortar businesses.

Weaknesses:

- The pay-to-play aspect of fan pages may create a challenge for your budget.
- Pages that used the simplified "Get Likes" feature now have a host of fans that will likely never become true fans.
- The youngest members of your target audience might be gravitating toward other platforms instead.

Twitter

Where users come to Facebook because they connect with friends, Twitter users seem to be most interested in their ability to connect to thought leaders and to become thought leaders themselves. While there is a level of friends following friends, Twitter users congregate more around shared interests and engage with those interests in real time. Twitter users break news, start movements, and seem willing to engage with complete strangers if the content of the tweet is interesting enough.

Audience: Twitter users are extremely active and tend to rely on a mix of hashtags and key thought leaders to stay engaged with the things they care about. Twitter may not be quite as expansive as Facebook in terms of demographics and audience size, but its audience is still huge and covers a wide range of topics. It's worth noting that

Twitter users tend to be a bit more tech-savvy than Facebook users, but like Facebook users, they tend to be most interested in B2C messaging or in C2C messaging.

Posting Tips:

- Know that unlike the Facebook feed, Twitter users see tweets in real time, so your followers are unlikely to see a tweet you made in the morning if they check their feeds at night.
- Plan to post with some frequency (two to three times a day at least).
- Use Favorites and Retweets to engage with leaders and fans in your industry.
- Leverage relevant hashtags to expose new audiences to your messaging.
- Avoid the mass-follow strategy when you try to grow your audience; you will likely end up with people more interested in having followers themselves than in buying what you sell.

Strengths:

- The potential reach of an interesting tweet can be huge.
- You can post a large volume of content without repercussions (in most cases).
- Hashtags give you an easy way to jump into the key conversations that your target prospects are having.
- Twitter's advertising platform is underrated.

Weaknesses:

- The volume of activity necessary for a successful Twitter platform can be difficult to maintain.
- If your audience is not tech savvy, they may be unlikely to use Twitter.
- Growing a profitable following can be difficult and time consuming.

Google+

In the social media world, Google+ is that weird cousin with completely normal, respectable, successful parents. Google+ boasts a huge user base, but critics have suggested that those numbers may be inflated by two factors:

Google accounts have become ubiquitous, and many people signed up for Google+ to see what it was and then stopped using it completely.

Those concerns aside, Google+ is hard to ignore because of Google's internet-wide reach. Everyone uses Google search. Gmail is popular as well. YouTube is a social media goliath. And Google has made efforts to tie all of its offerings together, with Google+ comprising one of those core pieces. On that front, it might be good for SEO but it is highly unlikely that you will build a meaningful audience on this platform, especially as Google shows signs of parting-out Google+ into individual services as the platform withers..

Audience: When you take into account its search engine optimization value (SEO, or how it affects your search engine ranking), Google+ is potentially connected to everyone that uses Google for search (3.5 billion searches per day, for some perspective). At the same time, the actual number of people using Google+ is difficult to estimate. For what it's worth, we have not met any business owner that has had any success with Google+. It seems to have a moderately engaged international audience, and a few key social media figures are boasting huge success on Google+. For the average social media marketer, however, Google+ appears to be a very fancy, well-funded ghost town.

Posting Tips:

- Maintaining a Google+ page seems to have value for SEO, which makes it worthwhile on some level for all businesses, especially if you have a physical location and can benefit from positive reviews.
- A moderate amount of activity, similar to Facebook seems to have a positive impact on your SEO.
- Tie your Google+ to your other Google properties, like your YouTube account to make it easier for your fans to find your other social accounts.

Strengths:

- Google likes Google, so if you can't find an audience on Google+ use it for SEO purposes.
- In general, the basic functionality of Google+ is similar to Facebook's, so repurposing your Facebook activity on Google+ should not be difficult.

- Google Maps tie-in makes a Google+ page valuable for brick and mortar businesses like shops and restaurants.
- Google Hangout functionality is a great way to host free live events or webinars (bonus: it can dump directly to YouTube).

Weaknesses:

- Your audience probably is not there.
- Over the last few years, Google has made numerous and frequent changes to the Google+ platform with little warning or explanation, so keeping up can be challenging.
- The platform might be a sinking ship.

YouTube

YouTube has become one of the most popular search engines in the world, and YouTube users are highly engaged. Content creators from all walks of life have found a home on YouTube, from once unknown vloggers to independent filmmakers to government leaders. If your messaging lends itself to video, YouTube can be a powerful way to engage fans. The platform integrates nicely with other Google offerings like Google AdWords and Google+, and the YouTube player itself is flexible enough that your content can live on YouTube but be embedded on your site. Furthermore, since YouTube welcomes unregistered users, unlike most social media platforms, the barrier for engaging with YouTube content is much lower than with other social networks.

Audience: Everyone that has an internet connection uses YouTube. B2B, B2C, C2C–it's all there. With over a billion users and a reported 100 hours of video uploaded every minute, YouTube is a bustling platform for everything and everyone. Make-up tutorials are just as common as construction tutorials, and independent or small business producers have achieved monumental success. At the same time, YouTube is so busy that it can be difficult to cut through the noise on quality alone, so you will probably need a strategy that encompasses more than just YouTube to get the most from your video content.

Posting Tips:

- The quality of your videos is more important than how frequently you post, but if you go for long stretches with no activity you should not expect your audience to grow.

- If your video editor offers YouTube specific export settings, use them to optimize the quality of your video (also great for reducing upload times).
- Fill out all of the details for your video (like title, description, category), and include a link back to your site in the description for SEO value.
- Flesh out your channel settings to make your page more appealing.
- Share your videos across your other platforms to drive traffic to your YouTube video.
- Avoid using copy-protected music and assets or risk having your videos taken-down.
- Keep back-ups of your videos in the event that your channel is compromised.

Strengths:

- Rich media is highly engaging, and YouTube is free to use.
- YouTube annotation functionality makes it easy for you to embed links and messages into your videos.
- The subscription functionality of YouTube helps you to maintain a following.
- YouTube integrates with Google AdWords, giving you another avenue to engage prospects.
- Hangout functionality lets you easily use YouTube as an archive tool for your live events.
- YouTube fields (like title, description, and category details) can be beneficial to SEO.

Weaknesses:

- Video can be expensive and time-consuming to develop.
- Learning to develop videos that reflect the same quality and poise of your business can be difficult.
- YouTube receives so much traffic that getting noticed from YouTube alone is impossible in most cases.

- YouTube users are ruthlessly cruel at times, so don't be surprised if you receive negative criticism.

LinkedIn

When it comes to B2B-focused social media sites, LinkedIn is the only game in town. LinkedIn started as a networking tool for professionals, free of the irrelevant (in the context of a professional relationship) frills that dominated more informal social networks like Facebook or MySpace.

Now, LinkedIn is working to become a hub for industry news and thought leadership, pushing content from a range of industries to the individuals that might find it interesting based on the information in their profiles. If at any point you cared about building your career, you probably made a LinkedIn profile–you and 300 million other professionals.

Audience: Because many LinkedIn users were creating profiles and only returning to the site when they needed to find a job, LinkedIn struggled to maintain consistent traffic. With the addition of a news feed and expanded interaction functionality, LinkedIn has started the journey of moving beyond being a digital rolodex for professional context. A large portion of the LinkedIn audience is still jobseekers, but more users are turning to LinkedIn for its potential to build thought leaders, adding a sizable portion of motivated and already-successful professionals to the mix as well.

Posting Tips:

- Your LinkedIn connections are likely very important business contacts, customers, or prospects, so be considerate of their time and attention.
- Posting frequently is not as important as it with other platforms, but sharing relevant high-quality information is.
- If you have a company page, don't expect to get a huge following from it; focus on the one-to-one relationships instead.
- Use your posts to maintain relationships. Comment on the posts other people make, and don't be afraid to send a message to catch-up.
- Like on Facebook, don't forget to edit the pre-populated attachment that appears when you share a link to make it more appealing to your audience.

- Take the time to connect with people you have just met, and take advantage of the "How You Met" journaling to remember key details about your connections.
- A high score on LinkedIn is meaningless if your connections don't know you and aren't interested in engaging with you or your business, so be selective about who you add.
- Find meaningful groups (that are more than just blog spam) to engage with.

Strengths:

- Ideal for B2B communications and one-to-one networking.
- Still primarily a recruiting tool.
- Can offer a more meaningful rolodex of key contacts, helping you to keep up with new developments in your network.
- Written recommendations are valuable relationship building tools and can be used as testimonials to help you attract new business.

Weaknesses:

- Many LinkedIn users are primarily interested in job opportunities, so marketing beyond that can be difficult.
- Company pages typically see low engagement from outsiders (but could be a valuable tool for building morale within your company).
- Cold-connections with LinkedIn prospects usually come off spammy, no matter how hard you try.

Pinterest

Pinterest as a social network struck upon a hidden niche in the social media world, and for some time many marketers ignored it, expecting Pinterest users to lose interest in the platform. Those marketers were wrong. To date, Pinterest drives more conversions than Facebook, Twitter , or Google+.

While these platforms at times drive more traffic, Pinterest users are much more willing to buy after jumping from Pinterest to your site. For this reason, Pinterest has become a vibrant content marketing platform. Unfortunately, the niche that makes Pinterest strong leaves almost all B2B businesses and a large number of B2C businesses on the outside looking in.

Audience: Pinterest users are largely young females interested in things like fitness, crafts, home-decorating, fashion, make-up, and feel-good messages. As Pinterest continues to grow, its users are maturing as well, so we are seeing less tech-savvy users, skewing slightly older, catching on to Pinterest's allure. Even with this growth, however, Pinterest is still light on male users and on businesses that don't fit the Pinterest aesthetic.

Posting Tips:

- Pinterest rewards quality as well as volume, so work to strike that balance with your audience.
- Follow Pinterest thought leaders relevant to your target audience, and re-pin their content frequently.
- Create worthwhile content that your audience is likely to share (based on what you see them sharing from other people in your space).
- Learn Pinterest copy conventions and what image styles seem to engage your users (approaches vary by topic, but longer photos tend to perform best).
- Engage your most active users to help spread your content, and don't be afraid to use your other social properties to drive interest in your in your Pinterest activity.
- If it's relevant for your business, consider using a Pinterest plugin to make it easier for Pinterest users to pin your website content.
- Fridays seem to be the best day for driving retail sales, so if that's your goal, post sales of your own products on Fridays.

Strengths:

- The all-star platform for e-commerce conversion.
- Pinterest lends itself to highly engaging visual content, making users attentive and active.
- Ideal for engaging a female audience.

Weaknesses:

- Can require a significant amount of time and energy to be effective.

- Growing an audience can be difficult, and even seeing traction from a single pin can take a month or more.
- Your audience may not use Pinterest.

Instagram

Instagram has somehow managed to balance mass market appeal with being one of the go-to haunts for the youngest demographics. Using Instagram is simple: take cool photos and write a caption. That simplicity combined with the low-stakes appeal of scrolling through hundreds of interesting pictures has made Instagram immensely successful.

You don't have to manage and curate a detailed profile like you do on Facebook and cope with all of the privacy concerns that come with that. Oh, and now you can shoot really simple short videos too, which is an easy way to manage the expectations that your audience might have with the quality of your videos.

Audience: The audience for Instagram tends to skew younger, but since the Facebook acquisition a wider variety of demographics are adopting the platform. As older consumers migrate to Instagram, the sheer volume of young users still cannot be overstated. Some users are even abandoning Facebook completely in favor of Instagram.

Posting Tips:

- Learn some photography basics and invest in a decent smartphone to ensure that the quality of your photos match the quality of your brand.
- Posting frequently won't hurt you as long as your photos are varied and interesting, so take the time to make your photos worthwhile.
- Load your photos up with relevant hashtags to pump your content into as many conversation streams as possible.
- Write clever captions to help bolster engagement with your photos.
- Get your customers involved. Try to take photos with happy customers if you can (be cautious with photographing children without release forms).
- Shoot quick videos from time to time, but be careful to stabilize the camera and avoid wind noise if you do (consider getting a smartphone tripod).

Strengths:

- Visual content like photos and short videos are highly engaging, making it ideal for a business that is highly visual by nature.
- The hashtag support on Instagram is ideal for getting in front of new customers.
- Instagram users seem more willing to engage with accounts that they are not familiar with than users on other networks.

Weaknesses:

- The challenge of growing an audience on Instagram is similar to that of Twitter, sometimes requiring significant time and effort.
- Having to take interesting photos day after day can be a deterrent to less creative or especially time-strapped business owners.
- If your brand does not naturally lend itself to being visual, Instagram will be a difficult platform to leverage.
- B2B business owners will find it difficult to market via Instagram.

Yelp

Yelp may not be a social platform in the same way that Facebook or Twitter is, but conversations about your business are likely happening there. In many ways, Yelp has become the new yellow pages but with reviews. Yelp has made itself valuable to businesses and consumers by making itself the middleman. Hungry and looking for a restaurant? Yelp can help. A restaurant looking for customers? Yelp can help.

Now, Yelp is struggling to maintain its status at the go-to resource for customers looking to find and try new things, but want to see some positive reviews before they take the plunge. Yelp in many ways has been a boon to brick and mortar locations from shops, to restaurants, to gyms, and has even begun to expand internationally. The downside: Yelp has been known to call businesses and offer to remove a bad review in exchange for a fee, and the influx of fake positive reviews is making consumers less trusting. As news like this spreads, consumers and business both seem to be growing leery of Yelp's quality and authenticity.

Audience: Yelp customers, by nature, tend to be shopping locally and are looking for places to visit. Sometimes they are tourists, and sometimes they are longtime residents looking to try something new. With a mobile app and an expansive website customers seem to be coming to Yelp from two directions, and the demographics of Yelp data cover nearly the entire spectrum of connected consumers.

Posting Tips:

- Flesh out your listing completely, aiming to answer all pertinent questions succinctly and effectively. Post your menu. Make sure your address is up to date. Include your website. List the phone number. Everything.
- Monitor for negative reviews, and avoid responding negatively. Instead, be humble and look to solve and defuse the problem.
- If you have a differentiator or a bestselling product or service, highlight it on your Yelp page.
- Share positive Yelp reviews across your other platforms and consider posting them on your website.
- Avoid paying for Yelp services like removing negative reviews or Yelp ads. Your budget is probably better invested in Facebook ads or Google AdWords.

Strengths:

- Yelp is like a large search engine for brick and mortar businesses.
- Many Yelp users are on mobile and are looking to make a purchasing decision relatively soon after their search.
- Your business listing offers a number of opportunities to showcase your offerings.
- Yelp users are inclined to leave reviews, so the platform can become a valuable archive of social proof.

Weaknesses:

- Some users are losing faith in Yelp and are migrating to apps like UrbanSpoon for recommendations.
- Yelp may ask for a fee to have a negative review removed.

Email

Like Yelp, many people might not consider email as being social media in the way that Facebook or Twitter are social media. For your purposes as a business owner or marketer, social media is any platform that allows you to engage in conversations directly with customers and prospects. In this way, email might be your most effective social media tool.

Historically, email marketing has some of the highest conversion rates of any marketing effort because it allows you to deliver a message to specific users that they are almost guaranteed to see. Because of this, digital marketers have been championing the value of an email list for years. And they're right. No matter what your business is, you should probably be trying to capture emails and use them to deliver company messaging.

Posting Tips:

- Make email capture a regular part of your sales efforts and consider offering freebies to entice people to opt-in even before the sale.
- As it is with all of your content, focus on delivering worthwhile messaging rather than a certain level of volume.
- Be creative with your email titles and with your content to capture interest.
- Pay careful attention to your metrics. Be mindful of over-contacting your email list.
- Clean out inactive subscribers from time to time to keep your metrics more accurate and more meaningful.
- Do not buy an email list. Grow yours organically.
- A/B test your email titles, images, and content to find the best approach for your audience.

Strengths:

- Email marketing boasts high engagement and conversion rates.
- The opt-in nature of email marketing tends to lead to more engaged users overall.
- You can use email capture to drive repeat conversions.
- If you build a smart sales funnel that includes email capture, you can track customer metrics from start to finish and find out who your best customers are.
- Email marketing is relatively cheap to maintain.

Weaknesses:

- The growth of email marketing and robust email management systems means that competition for inbox intention is higher than ever.
- You might need to invest in some graphic design to make your emails more effective.
- Gaming your email list to find the best styles of titles and the best body content for clicks and conversions can be tedious.
- Audiences are becoming more guarded with their email addresses, so you may have to work harder to earn your emails.
- Frequent emails can quickly feel spammy.

Other

Social media marketing is evolving every day, and though we covered the largest platforms in this e-book, there are a number of platforms that we didn't discuss. For example, we didn't discuss Snapchat, Slideshare, Delicious, Ustream, Periscope, Snapchat, FourSquare, Flickr, or podcasting.

The beauty of social media is that a variety of audiences are congregating in different places to discuss and share their interests. Just because a platform isn't a mega-player in the space on par with Facebook or Twitter doesn't mean that you should discount it. If your audience is using it, you should probably consider using it as well.

About the Author

Marshal D. Carper

As a kid, I never really fit in, and I used to think that was my greatest weakness.

Now, as an author, content marketing consultant, and business owner, I realize that not fitting in is actually my greatest strength. While the rest of an industry chases the trends, I strive to lead my businesses and my clients to capture untapped opportunities. We learn from the best practices of the space and develop an "outside of the box" strategy that allows us to compete from a different angle.

While everyone else crowds the front door, we sneak in the side door.

I used this approach to get my first book published, to found Artechoke Media through crowdfunding, and to establish a competitive edge for Synersteel Studio. For my clients, this has meant a 3X increase in sales during pivotal months for one, a 47 percent increase in retention for another, and a 25 percent subscription increase in a highly competitive B2B service space for another (to name a few).

If you're like me and you don't mind not fitting in, let's work together. We could build something special.

Made in the USA
Lexington, KY
17 April 2018